GENETTE IS MISSING

GENETTE IS MISSING

By her father John W Tate

DAVID & CHARLES
Newton Abbot London North Pomfret (VT)

ISBN : 0 7153 7907 0
Library of Congress Catalog Card Number

© John W Tate, 1979

All rights reserved. No part of this
publication may be reproduced, stored
in a retrieval system, or transmitted,
in any form or by any means, electronic,
mechanical, photocopying, recording or
otherwise, without the prior permission
of David & Charles (Publishers) Limited

Set in 10 on 12 Times
and printed in Great Britain
by Wheatons Ltd, Exeter, Devon
for David & Charles (Publishers) Limited
Brunel House Newton Abbot Devon

CONTENTS

1	Genette is Missing	7
2	False Alarms	28
3	The Search Widens	46
4	UFOs	72
5	The Psychic Researchers	82
6	The Occult Detectives *Colin Wilson*	100
7	Where is Genette now?	141
8	International Find a Child	150

1 Genette is Missing

Why should I want to write such a book?

On Sunday, 3 September 1978, I received a short note delivered to my home by a well-meaning person:

> We all send out our thoughts to you and are doing all we can to help the police. The church service today will bring great power to the village of Aylesbeare, although you may not believe in it at this moment.

On reading that little note my first feeling was one of anger. What right had anyone to question my beliefs? That first emotionial reaction was soon replaced with feelings of sorrow that this person should believe that great power only existed at odd times. Did they not realise that power is there waiting to be tapped at all times, not just when we gather together in large numbers?

From that moment on, however, I realised people could learn a great deal from my experiences and feelings and that few actually could even imagine the happenings and events leading up to that Sunday and the things that have happened since.

Where to begin? I was always brought up to start at the beginning so, as this story is really about a little lost girl, let's first talk about that little girl. Description issued Monday, 21 August 1978:

> 13-year-old Genette Louise Tate of Barton Farm Cottage, Aylesbeare is 5ft tall, with short brown hair and brown eyes, is suntanned and looks her age.

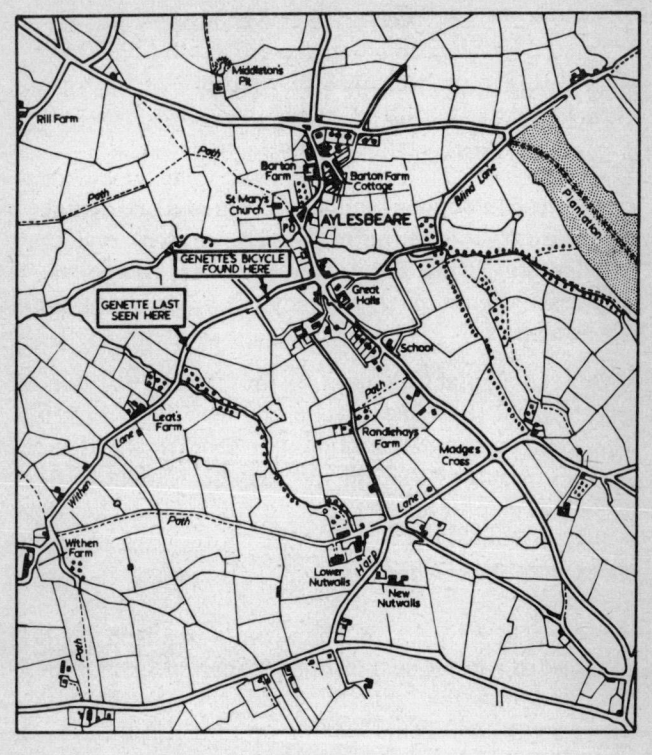

When she disappeared Genette was wearing a white cotton high round-necked top with the name 'GENETTE' embroidered in red about 5 inches long on the left shoulder. She was also wearing brown trousers and white plimsolls.

'Ginny', as we know her, was born 5 May 1965 with a tooth and at the time was quite a VIP and a rather painful problem to her mother! She suffered from colic for the first three months of her life, talked at nine months and walked at eighteen months, but she was bald until she was two years old and was then suddenly blessed with a crop of beautiful curls. Her inquisitiveness began at an early age. I well remember her scrutinizing a worm in the garden when she was two.

She started school at five and began to show great interest and curiosity about everything she came into contact with. From an early age her ability in mental arithmetic amazed us all in the family. She was happy at school and looked forward to it every day.

At eleven she set off to attend the largest comprehensive school in the country at Exmouth. Her desire to learn helped her to overcome her natural shyness and she developed a keen interest in most things. Her best subjects were French, Maths and English. She enjoyed writing and composing poetry. Her school report at the end of July 1978 was a joy to read.

Like all children she often talked about what she wanted to do when she grew up, including nursing and police work (although she thought she would not be tall enough for this); for a long time she definitely decided that she wanted to become a vet, but after watching the TV serial 'All Creatures Great and Small' she changed her mind abruptly. She had a love of the countryside and the creatures that lived in it. Her virtues were patience, willingness to help and an ability to overcome difficulties with her gorgeous smile.

So to that dreadful day — Saturday, 19 August 1978. At 7.30am I left the house with my wife Violet (Genette's step-mother) to take her to work in the local hospital. Then I went on to get some petrol, before going to the doctor's surgery at Woodbury (I had a sore throat) where I sat quietly waiting for 9am, reading the daily newspaper. Just before 9 o'clock the doctor arrived. I was second in line and at 9.20 it was my turn. After a brief interview and examination I returned home, arriving at about 10am. From upstairs I could hear excited chatter from Tania and Genette (Tania is Genette's step-sister) as Tania was making her final arrangements to go on her fortnight's holiday with her father. I started to get breakfast and shouted upstairs for them to come down.

Breakfast was eaten and cleared away. The girls briskly set about dressing, darting here and there, a quick run to the village Post Office for some sweets and then eventually Tania was ready to go. Genette by this time had settled in the garden on a blanket working on her much read and dog-eared puzzle books. It was a lovely day: the sun was shining, everyone was happy — all doing the things they wanted to.

At 12.20pm Tania, her boyfriend, David, and I set off to collect Julie, Tania's young friend (whom we had nicknamed Lydia because she reminded us all of the girl in the TV serial) and on into Exeter, where we collected Violet at the end of her morning's work. We saw many cars on the way, full of happy people on their way to their holidays.

When we all arrived at the coach station it too was humming with activity, with the dozens of extra coaches laid on to cope with the enormous influx of holiday visitors at this time of the year. The heavy traffic had delayed the coaches but eventually Tania's arrived and the scramble began — only four seats the driver said. The girls left us to handle the baggage and so were fortunate enough to get two of the four seats.

Those who failed to get a seat wandered to and fro, not knowing quite what to do or where to go; then along came the relief coach and all were happy. At 3.10pm the coach pulled out while we waved goodbye. I remember thinking that Genette would be on her paper-round by now, merrily cycling along the country lanes, breathing in good clean country air, well away from the grime and thick diesel fumes we were battering our lungs with. Then another picture flashed through my mind — Vault Beach in Cornwall, beachcombing with the sea trickling between and over my toes. Oh how my heart aches at times to return to Cornwall and the peaceful life we lived there three years ago!

After the coach had left, Violet and I attended to a chore in a nearby shop, ate an icecream and then drove gently home — we were in no hurry. As we passed the airport we saw the Spanish airlines jet on the tarmac spewing out its load of holidaymakers returning from Palma and our conversation turned to our own dream holiday to be taken later in the year, and the quiet fortnight ahead. Soon we were home for an English cup of tea.

Then the nightmare began. I had parked the car — Vi came rushing to me with Genette's bicycle, followed by Tracey — a friend of Genette's — who was trying very quickly to tell us that Genette was nowhere to be found. And so the search began. Up and down Within Lane. Was she here? Was she there? Had she been to this house or that one? We knocked at every house we came to. Meanwhile the village lads were scrambling over hedges and around the fields. After what seemed like hours Vi said, 'Go to the police!' We checked home first and then we went to see Constable Laws, the policeman in the village. What should be done? The panic had set in. We phoned the Exeter Police Headquarters and told the story again. 'Go home', they said, 'and wait.' We went home. The phone was ringing as we opened the door. 'Where is the bike?' 'Here', I said. And then through the window I saw the first of the boys in blue with the police dogs.

From our windows you can see the spot where Ginny's bicycle was found. But where was she now? Then the police started to arrive. The quick efficient questioning, finding out what they needed to know. Desperate searches through drawers for this piece of information or that. Had she run away before? If she had, where would she go? All the time we felt sure she hadn't.

As the day dragged on the sound of a helicopter very low overhead made us all rush outside. What a fantastic feeling that was! A warm tingle ran up my spine. What a country we live in. No other country in the world, I felt, would bother so much or act so fast. You could even feel the vibration indoors, it was so close. To and fro, to and fro, and yet NOTHING!

Slowly darkness began to fall and with it the rain. I imagined Genette staggering in a daze — the rain having woken her up somewhere. So I drove around and around, country lane after country lane. Once when I got back to the village I met a group of people who were searching in the darkness with only two torches. Oh God let the rain stop! I pleaded. Eventually we realised that it was pointless to continue in the darkness. We lay on the bed to rest until first light: it was already 3.30am. The rain stopped — my prayers had been answered.

Just before 5am we made a cup of tea and went out again. First one part of the common, then another, then back to Within Lane. Perhaps the still of the morning would tell us something fresh. *No — nothing!* Then back up to the common. We searched around all the obvious parking spots. After a while we began to feel hungry and realised we hadn't eaten for nearly twenty-four hours, so home we went for food. We found that the food seemed to have no taste and it was just like chewing cardboard, but we forced ourselves — feeling that we ought to eat to keep our strength up.

Someone came to tell us that there was to be an organised search by the police and villagers. We decided that I should stay by the phone and Vi should go on the search as I probably would not be able to walk far enough or fast enough (I suffer from muscular dystrophy). So the first search of the district, that was to become a daily occurrence, began.

During the morning Genette's mother, Sheila, rang to say she was coming. We had parted when Genette was four-and-a-half years old but in recent years we had allowed the past to be forgotten and become friends for the benefit of Genette. Although Sheila and I were apart we still shared a common love for Genette and now the tears flowed. I had held them back until now, but suddenly I was overwhelmed with a total feeling of inadequacy realising that by this time Genette could be absolutely anywhere and that even with the hundreds of people helping us to look, the task of finding her was so enormous.

The police arrived again to take longer, fuller statements: more questions, more searches. Friends arrived to comfort us. The helicopter searched again, but still nothing.

So the waiting began. We felt as though we were in a daze. Sunday just turned into Monday. The days seemed unimportant but we counted them and made use of every second to the full.

Monday brought the Press and television in force. After our first TV interviews we were faced with the awesome task of having to attend a Press conference. We were frightened of the reporters at first but with the never-ending support and help of the police we coped, even though at one time it needed the strong arm of the law to retain our privacy, and the garden gate was almost demolished. We did two TV interviews, one after the other; during the first we just felt stunned, but the second was an awful experience with our tears welling and fear and emotion overwhelming us. Then more searching; there was always somewhere new to look. Darkness fell and once again we had to stop.

By now we had lost track of the days and in fact at one time we had to scratch them out on the calendar to know where we were. We were in a continuous daze and hurry: visits to the police, searching, trying to eat, trying to snatch a bit of sleep when we could stand up no longer. Yet all the time we had hope and would not allow ourselves to feel defeated. No task was impossible. If we could not do it, someone else would.

Our days began at dawn — 5am. We got up and made a cup of tea, then drove to the GPO sorting office to collect the mail just in case. Any letters we didn't recognise we handed to the police for scrutiny. After an early morning visit to the Police Incident Centre (set up in the Village Hall) we would return home to cook breakfast. Then a journey to buy the newspapers; soon we had more than at the newsagents. Then a discussion as to where to search that day and off we would go.

On Wednesday we intended to search every inch of the road from the Village Hall to the airport, this being a route that someone abducting her might have used. We hoped that Genette might have thrown something out of a car for us to find. One of us always had to stay behind to answer the phone, but neither of us wanted to be left at home on our own. We were scared of the unknown.

So, slowly the search progressed, going carefully along the verges and hedgerows, prodding every pile of leaves, flicking up every piece of paper, turning over every bit of polythene. It surprises you how much litter is left lying around, particularly polythene bags, when you have to examine every piece of it. The weather was hot and our feet felt as if they were on fire. Our trusty sticks were becoming more and more smooth with continual use.

By Wednesday night we had got halfway to the airport. We were desperately overtired, both physically and mentally. We continually racked our brains for any possible clues. Then the first row blew up, followed by terrible soul-searching. Was any one of us to blame? Had she run away because she was unhappy and we hadn't known? Had we ever done enough for her? Had we made other things more important? Had we talked to her enough? Why hadn't we cuddled her more? Why hadn't we done this or that? So the questions came, followed by the tears of desperation and the quiet prayers for forgiveness. We slowly began to see just how trivial the day-to-day occurrences of the world are.

How petty those moments at work seemed, when we got all wound up and angry. We felt that for once in our lives we could see things in perspective. Nothing was as important as Genette or the family. We all agreed that never again would we allow the home or family or ourselves to take second place to anything or anybody outside. We should work to provide leisure time, and our leisure time should be our real life.

The arguments continued and the tension rose until even to be in the house was unbearable. Someone said the police should be told the substance of our arguments — I grabbed at this excuse to leave.

My coat was on and I was out of the door in no time at all. I wandered up the road, my mind in a state of bewilderment. Had we all contributed in some way to make Ginny run away? Why had she gone without taking anything with her if this was so? Even though the facts made it improbable that she had run away, slowly I began to wonder. We had tried to keep an open mind all along as to what had happened to her but had we really considered every possibility?

At the door of the Incident Centre someone asked how I was and got me a cup of coffee and sat me down. We talked about all sorts of things and my sanity returned. 'What wonderful people these policemen are', I thought, but then what I was going through was a once-in-a-lifetime nightmare, whereas they must meet such problems almost daily. After a while someone came looking for me and we walked back down the road to the house.

I slept that night through sheer exhaustion.

On Thursday morning we found we were able to plan our time properly and make better use of every available minute. Another Press conference came and went.

Then we were back to the search.

Towards late afternoon we reached the area near the airport. We went around the area to the right of the road and, with each step we took, we became more and more alarmed. During the last war the airfield had been used by the Americans and a good deal of the evidence of their wartime presence remained behind. Amazingly the place was open to anyone to wander into. There were open manhole covers to catch your feet, broken-down buildings to hide anything, underground bunkers piled with filth and rubbish from goodness knows where, water storage ponds, old loo blocks and chimney stacks; it was too much for our imagination. Why was it all still here? The war was over more than thirty years ago.

This place was beyond us; it needed to be searched systematically. We decided to leave it to the police dogs. We walked away feeling outraged. If only it had been flattened and the bunkers filled in, or even wired off, our fears need not have been so great. Why do we allow this beautiful countryside of ours to get into such a state? Why do we ruin it with our continual dumping of waste. Everywhere we searched we found the rejected cast-offs of a material society.

We returned home to find yet another search of the house in progress by the police, but somehow it all seemed less offensive and easier to cope with now. Our hysteria had died down, our tears had gone, we were ready to fight and for as long as it took. We thought positively amongst ourselves, not allowing negative thoughts or ideas even to creep into our minds and, amazingly, we found a new form of energy to sustain us.

I went to the church that evening and prayed.

A simple statement one might think but it seemed like an eternity since I had last been at peace with God. I had forgotten that, regardless of my past life, He was still there waiting to help me. I asked for His guidance and help, not just for me but for everyone involved in the task of searching for Genette. The feelings of quietness and patience that came then have been with me since; that power is there to help us if only we could learn to tune into it and draw from it in our day-to-day lives. Someone once said: 'What have I to fear with God on my side?' How right that statement feels, but how seldom we relate it to our day-to-day lives. I feel that one of the biggest mistakes we all make is to think of religion as something that applies to Sundays only and that the church, with its pomp and ceremony has perhaps encouraged this attitude. We should worship as we live life — continuously. Then I ask myself who am I to talk like this with all the things I have done in my life; but perhaps it is because of my past that I am what I am and think the way that I do.

Just before dark we went back to the airport area to check some of the old buildings on the other side of the road. There was also an old caravan there which we looked over. As we came away we were startled by the noise of something moving over an old sheet of galvanised iron lying in the entrance to one of the bunkers. Our minds all jumped to the same thing at once. 'Ginny', I called out, and stood and waited. There was no reply. I tried again but it was in vain. We decided it was probably a rabbit and made our way sadly back to the car and then home.

Thursday became Friday. My brother Ken arrived in the morning. He was quite a stranger, having only recently returned from Germany with the RAF. He was every inch the military policeman and it gave us a feeling of security to have him around. We sat in the front garden and talked about old times and discussed the many theories we had about Ginny's disappearance.

During the afternoon we had a new challenge to face up to with the arrival of Colin Wilson, the author, who brought with him Bob Cracknell — the psychic. Mr Cracknell was a most unusual man: bronzed and extremely fit and healthy — but to me his most prominent features were his eyes. Immediately I felt that here was a man who was completely at ease with himself, and had a great understanding of the world about him. He had been out to Within Lane. He had also had contact with things belonging to Ginny and now he wanted to talk to Violet on her own. While she talked I chatted with Colin. I had met him once before some years ago whilst working for the Youth Club at Gorran Haven in Cornwall. I had come to know his family quite well, particularly his daughter, and on the wall of our sitting-room was a picture that she had drawn for us, which I naturally showed him as he had never seen it before.

Time went by and we realised that Bob Cracknell had been talking to Vi for quite a time. Eventually he came down the stairs and departed, saying that he would see me soon. Vi was rather distressed and she had obviously been crying. We did not know at the time what had upset her. She could not explain why and said that they had only talked about things in general.

One of her main worries at this time was that Tania would not be allowed to come home. She was afraid that she would be kept away from the house whilst Genette was still missing.

In reality Bob Cracknell was just the first of many,

each with their own theory; later we were to be inundated with theories.

I had been feeling ill all that day, aching all over most of the time and feeling very cold and shivery. I had been using Niagara Therapy equipment for a considerable time to ease the pain from my muscles. I went and lay down for a few hours' rest in the late afternoon to find that even I was to have 'psychic' dreams. I had been lying very still and quiet for a while but the room around me seemed to be full of mist and emptiness. I was neither asleep nor awake when suddenly I pictured very clearly in my mind a blue MGB sports car with a black drophead. Then the scene changed and I was looking at a ruined castle tower with ivy creeping up the walls. Part of the wall had crumbled away and one could see the large blocks of stone. There were several of these scattered around. The tower was incomplete on one side but stood almost to its full height on the other. Then the scene flashed through my mind of a large waterfall with its sparkling cascade of water travelling ever onwards with keen, clear, crystal brightness.

It was round about this time that we noticed the pets were behaving rather unusually — our cat, Mouser, in particular. Mouser was normally a wandering sort of creature; he had been a farm animal and was allowed a lot of natural freedom. He liked to be let out in the morning and would usually be gone until darkness, hunting rabbits or mice through the grass which surrounded us, for he had easy access to the fields and no roads to frighten him. Yet since Genette had been gone he hadn't left the house. We noticed that whenever we did anything, whether we were looking through a cupboard or whatever we were doing, Mouser was with us. He was never very far away. It almost seemed at times that he was speaking to us. Tammy, our spaniel cross dog, was obviously pining. She mooned about the place, wandering to and fro, never content. She was missing her daily walks with Genette. She was becoming deafer and her brown eyes were even sadder than usual; being an old dog she had her problems.

The police searches continued. We had now entered the seventh day. Various things had taken place. Police horses had been brought down from Bristol and had been searching parts of the nearby commons. Someone had seen a silver-grey mini speeding away from Aylesbeare on that Saturday and a hue and cry began on the Friday evening to try to find this particular vehicle. The *Express & Echo* newspaper — the one that Genette had been delivering when she disappeared — were the first people to come forward to offer £1,000 reward for information leading directly to the safe return of Genette. They printed thousands of handbills with a picture of Genette on them which gave details relating to the reward and a police telephone number. Many of these posters were to be about for a long long time after that.

We were overwhelmed by this offer of a reward because it was something that we just could not have afforded. When we were first told about it, at the Friday morning Press conference, we could not control our emotions.

Later we heard that the mini the police had been looking for had been traced and had no connection whatsoever with Genette's disappearance, and so another of the possible leads was eliminated. That night an appeal was made by the police to Devon people and holidaymakers to give up seven hours over the bank holiday to look for Genette. They wanted to carry out an extensive search of Woodbury Common — an area that we had spent many hours searching the previous Sunday, talking to people, showing them Genette's photograph, asking them if they had seen her and walking over large areas of it. We had searched as much as we could but the size of the common made our efforts inadequate. The police had searched there too with horses and had decided that the only way to do it thoroughly was to get as many people as possible onto the common to check it yard by yard all over again. The appeal went out by television, radio and newspapers for people to come forward to give up their time. So Friday went and Saturday arrived. A week had gone — the first of many.

We look back now at the cuttings taken from the newspapers and see almost with amusement the headline in the *Express & Echo* on that night: 'The Police throw cordon around Village in Genette Hunt' — that was one week after she went missing! Even in our desperation then, we felt that the thorough search should have been carried out a week previously. However, the police then set up checkpoints on all the minor roads leading out of Aylesbeare and teams of detectives and uniformed police questioned everybody — only briefly if they were villagers, but at some length if they were people from outside the area who had not been seen before. The hope was that the holidaymakers who had passed through the week before would be passing the same way a week later on their way home and might have information.

The search continued throughout the day while arrangements were being made for the big search on the Sunday. We ourselves worked out what we were going to do on the Sunday and then, just after lunch, we had the second visit from Bob Cracknell. The house was full of friends who were offering their help, when he arrived. He came in and sat down in the sitting-room with everyone around him and fired questions at us. What did we think had happened? We had to face up to the truth. Either she was alive or she was dead. If she was alive she had run away. If she was dead — well goodness knows what had happened. One got the impression at times that when you were talking to this man, no one else could hear you. Whether it was so or not, I don't know. As he was about to leave he said the only thing he could say to us was that it would all be over by the Sunday and he prayed to God that we would have the strength to cope with it. We asked him where we should look, where we should go? He stood in our lounge and pointed and said, 'If you go *that* way, about five miles, you will find a wood where you will find something of interest'.

After he had gone we set off in the direction he had pointed. I drove as far as I could in the right general direction until we came to a right-angled bend in the road where, to the left, was a bridleway. My instincts told me to follow it. Unfortunately the water running downhill during the winter had cut a deep channel across the track so we could drive no further. We all piled out.

There was myself and Violet, her brother, who had spent some time in the army, and her sister. We had the dog with us and we decided to let her go off the lead to see if she could pick up any scent. We had in our minds the idea that we were following a track that Genette had made on foot.

The bridleway continued between two fields with

high hedges on either side and then it narrowed to a footpath. We were gently going uphill. Every step we took, the dog's tail became more excited as she rushed ahead with her nose to the ground. Our spirits began to rise as we felt that here was something at last. The going was now becoming harder. We were climbing very steeply in places and alongside the path was a rugged gully which the winter rain had cut while making its rapid descent down the hillside. Our progress was now very slow: in places it was so steep that we had to help one another along. The brambles were overgrown to such a degree that at times we were almost crawling through a tunnel of leaves. And still the dog was plunging ahead. We chatted excitedly together as we found one possible clue after another.

Along the way we noticed hazelnut shells on the ground, sweet papers here and there and also ears of corn that had been eaten. To us it appeared just the sort of trail Genette would have left, for she loved the country and knew how to live off it.

We travelled in this manner uphill for a mile and a half. The dog was still plodding on. She was convinced she was on the scent of something, and she was, for eventually we came to the source. It turned out to be a squirrel's nest. The squirrel had obviously been foraging over a wide area for nuts for its store.

We did not give up but decided to continue to see where the path eventually came out. The ground was now less steep and as it levelled out the track widened until we came out of the wooded part and on to another bridlepath. This path went along the bottom of someone's garden. We looked over the hedge and saw several white rabbits loose on the lawn. We immediately thought that Genette would certainly have been attracted to these rabbits and quite possibly would have gone over the fence to look at them. In another field nearby we came across a wooden shed containing hay. Someone had been around it — there was no doubt about that: the high grass all around it had been flattened, most probably by someone looking for Genette.

And so we continued until we came to a road which we followed for a quarter of a mile to a point where another footpath went off to the left up the side of a wooded hill and this was the track we followed. To the left the wood was thick with pines as far as one could see; to the right was gorse and bracken. Ahead the stony pathway climbed quite quickly. We slowly reached the top; everyone else was there before me as by now I was becoming very weary.

We later discovered that we had climbed to the top of Beacon Hill, one of the highest spots for miles around. The magnificent view from this majestic place made us feel humble and small — to look for a human being down there below was like looking for a needle in a haystack. We felt hopelessly inadequate. From our vantage point we could see the sea in one direction, while behind us was what seemed an unending ridge of pine forest stretching into the distance.

By this time dusk was beginning to catch up with us and we thought if we were to make it back before dark we would really have to get moving so we started the long trek back down the hill. Darkness came swiftly and we had no torches. It was spooky to say the least. We made the descent quite speedily for our nerves were not as good as they normally were.

We scrambled and slipped and slid until we eventually got to the bottom and back to the car.

We felt disappointed, tired and dejected and yet there was the dog still busily wagging her tail and thoroughly enjoying every minute of the expedition.

We were now getting worried as we had left Sheila at home and we thought she would be concerned about us still searching after dark and wondering if we had fallen or hurt ourselves or something, although we needn't have been. She had guessed what we had been up to and was not at all panicky when we eventually got to a telephone box, and rang to say that we were on our way and to put the kettle on!

We got back to the house and discussed what we had seen and decided the next thing we should do was to get hold of a map. We had followed Bob Cracknell's direction basically by intuition but to do it properly we needed to work the thing out by using a map and compass. That was Saturday. It had been a very busy day on the whole.

We got up on Sunday morning and went up to the Incident Centre to find out what we were going to be allowed to do during the big search and were greeted by one of the policemen who said that he thought it would be a good idea if I went with them into the police station to go over some of the statements in case I could sort out some things for them. I waited around for a while and off we went. I did not realise then that this was to be the day that they would question me fully. I was like an animal trapped in a cage all the time I was in that police station; the only place I wanted to be was out with the many many people who had turned up for the search. I paced the room quite a bit. I wanted to get out. The day dragged on. We went over every bit of the Saturday's happenings, from the time I got up for breakfast, right through the day. When lunchtime came they took me out for a meal and on the way I drove them round to show them where I had parked my car, where we had sat and eaten an icecream and so on. After lunch, back to the police station, this time to write up the statement. I was tired and beginning to fall asleep and they said, 'For goodness sake keep awake! We need you!'

At about 5 o'clock in the evening they dropped me back home. I was completely shattered. The search by then had practically come to an end. My brother and his wife had been out all day along with many other friends. Altogether some seven thousand people had been searching for Genette. 'Genette's welly army', as one of the papers dubbed them the following day: 'Like a massive army of ants marching across the fields'. But yet again a blank was drawn. Most of the areas the people had been searching had already been covered before by the police. It was just a way of making absolutely certain that nothing had been missed.

Where did we go from there? All these people helping and still no sign of Genette. We felt pretty desperate, sad and very, very disappointed. Sunday had been and gone with no result. But Bob Cracknell was wrong — it was not over.

2 False Alarms

We were now able to cope with the days much more easily than we had been. The nights — well that was a different matter. At night our thoughts turned to horror. We were scared to put out the lights so we had them on all night throughout the entire house. Also the lights outside were on in case Genette should return home or the police come to fetch us in a hurry.

Our fears really stemmed from one night early on. We had gone to bed and were dozing when suddenly I was awakened by the slamming of a car door. I was out of bed, trousers on, down the stairs and out of the front door as quick as a flash. Once in the front garden my eyes searched the lawns and hedges in haste. I looked for anything that might have changed since I had checked around it just before going to bed. Nothing. I went out through the front gate and up the road alongside the house, searching the verges as I went. Nothing. Then into the back garden through the wooden side gate. I swept the torch beam around, along the vegetable rows, into the log shed. I pushed open the door of the outside loo. Still nothing. I turned around and went back down the road and into the front garden. Then I saw something under the kitchen window. What seemed to be a bag with a stone in the bottom of it that had been thrown over the hedge — at least that was my first impression on seeing it there. I took one look and decided that the police had better be called. As I was still a bit drowsy and confused, I forgot completely that

I could telephone the police and set off at a run. I cannot run very far — in fact I only got as far as my car before I was out of breath so I scrambled into the car and drove to the Incident Centre where I told the police my story. They immediately came out of the Centre and piled into my car and we came back down the road to the house.

They followed me into the garden, bringing with them a big communications radio which sat bleeping away in the middle of the lawn. The time was now 3.30am. One of the policemen was pretty certain that the vehicle we had heard had been their panda car and he was busily trying to make contact with it to make certain of this. Meanwhile we investigated the bag. It turned out to be a Mother's Pride bread bag which had some earth inside it or something similar (it could have been stale bread). We came to the conclusion that it had probably been dragged there by a hedgehog as they were often in the garden at night rummaging noisily along the border edge. The police decided to check the rest of the garden, the outbuildings and so on for any other signs of disturbance.

Meanwhile a call came back from the panda car to confirm that, while driving away from the Incident Centre, he had left his car door open and, as he got to our house, he had slammed it to close it. This was obviously the noise I had heard.

The police returned to the Incident Centre. We made a cup of tea and waited for dawn which was only an hour away. This episode unnerved us and we became frightened of the night from that moment onwards — not frightened of the dark but of what our imaginations conjured up in the dark.

We put out the bedroom light to create a semi-darkness, which made it possible to doze off, but in this half awake, half asleep state we could not stop our minds from going over all the terrible possibilities that could have happened, conjuring up pictures of some of the hair-raising stories we had been told.

One such story told to Sheila, for example, was about a father who, after a long and arduous search through many backstreet establishments, had found his daughter in a filthy room, lying on a bed. She had been heavily drugged and treated despicably by all and sundry. Her mind was in such a state of confusion that when her father entered the room she tried to climb up the wall to escape yet another onslaught.

Then there were the various stories told of how to dispose of a body. These tales of evil and blackness were amongst the strongest tests of my faith: I knew in my heart that even if Genette was dead she would be with someone who loved her dearly — my mother. She died at the age of fifty from cancer when Genette was four, but no grandmother could have cared more for her than she did. My faith in life after death continued to give me the strength I needed to fight against the thoughts that clouded my mind during the long hours of darkness in the quietness of my room at night.

Naturally we thought of all sorts of horrible things that could have happened to Genette. At times we fell asleep almost repeating to ourselves, 'Where, oh where is she? Please let it be tomorrow that we find her'. The night-time fear was so great as far as Violet was concerned that if she wanted to go to the loo downstairs in the middle of the night, I would have to accompany her. She was terrified of going downstairs on her own. In the daytime the signs of stress were such that if someone spoke loudly or the telephone rang, she would jump.

We were still in a state of confusion, not knowing what or who we were up against. Sometimes at night, after we got back into the habit of going to bed properly again, we would both get undressed, carefully putting our clothes into the right order of dress to facilitate getting up in a hurry if we were called out in the middle of the night. Then we would stand by the side of the bed frozen to the spot, frightened to get into it. I am still unable to understand just what our fears were but I do know that until this happened I did not know what it was like to be really frightened.

After a few days of this sort of occurrence I began to realise what people had meant in the past when they had said that they were frightened of something or another. How I wished that I had taken more notice of them at that time and had been able to comfort them with a friendly word and a kind thought to help them on their way.

Fear had been a constant companion since Genette's disappearance. This awesome enemy is never far away, waiting to take over our minds at every possible opportunity. If for a moment we allow our thoughts to drift, instead of consciously planning our mental activities and keeping our minds fully occupied, we cannot exclude the fear. Fear seems to have no manners or courtesy and barges in at the most unexpected times. The most commonplace things trigger it off: an odd word in conversation, a minute's unpunctuality, even a mole hill in a green field. We found all these could reduce us from cool calmness to absolute panic in a few seconds. Fear is powerful and destructive if we allow it to take over our minds.

We found that, as the days went by, we had to learn to protect each other. We never went anywhere on our own and always made sure our whereabouts were known — even to the extent of letting the police know when we went shopping. In fact we went nowhere without their knowledge. We also had to learn not to jump up quickly from a chair, or react swiftly, or make sudden movements in any way, so as to prevent the other from being thrown into an immediate panic. So, slowly, we began to learn a new art — the control of fear. Fear of the unknown. Basically fear is an attitude of mind; all we did was to learn to change our thought patterns, the most important one being not to accept any theory or idea without the facts to substantiate it. Even the most bizarre stories usually have been found to have quite logical interpretations, although sometimes needing long and arduous investigation.

On Monday, 28 August, it was Violet's turn to be questioned by the police. She was collected at 9.30 in the morning and taken into the police station. We sent her complete with a thermos flask of tea. I remembered what it had been like the day before with no drinks available and this being Bank Holiday Monday their canteen would be closed and, as Vi loves her cup of tea, we felt it wrong for her to go without.

That same day I had been out earlier in the morning and bought a Silva compass and an ordnance survey map of the district to enable us to do another search of the area Bob Cracknell had referred to. I came back to the house and busily set about establishing just where the location was that he had been on about. We had the map spread out on the sitting-room floor and, using a pair of dividers, we drew a circle with a five-mile radius, Aylesbeare Village Hall being the centre point. Then using the compass we took a bearing in the direction in which Bob Cracknell had pointed. This gave us a more precise idea of where we were supposed to be looking. Throughout this operation the doorbell kept ringing with one interruption after another. The press wanting to talk about this or that; the police wanting to eliminate yet another pair of shoes. (Every piece of clothing found in the area was brought to us for possible identification.)

Eventually we set off by car and, to our utter amazement, found ourselves within fifty yards of where we had been the Saturday before.

During the Press conference on that day the police released information that they had obtained from a mother and daughter who had been walking in Within Lane. They remembered stopping and talking to the three girls and then continuing on their way. Minutes later a maroon car driven by a young dark-haired man had passed them going towards the girls. The police with their help had produced a photofit picture of the young man and this was issued to the Press. The young man whom the police were anxious to trace might not have been involved but even so he might have seen something and the police very much wanted to talk to him.

Later on in the afternoon, at about 5 o'clock, Violet arrived back from the police station, having been through a day's questioning. We had our evening meal, walked up to the Village Hall to see if there was any news from the police (this had now become a twice-daily routine) and then home again to a final check around the garden and that was our Bank Holiday Monday over.

The following morning Sheila was asked to go to the police station in Exeter for her session of questioning.

We were also told that the Rev Denis Large would like to see us all in the afternoon at the Rectory at Clyst St George. Sheila returned just after midday and at 3 o'clock that afternoon we made our way to Clyst St George. We arrived early and decided to take a walk around the church, which is next to the Rectory.

This little country church is a perfect example of how modern building can be made to blend with its surroundings. On 31 August 1940, almost all but the typical red Devon tower was destroyed by fire. The Clyst St George area was heavily showered by incendiary bombs, one of which found its way inside the organ. On the following morning only the tower and part of the perimeter walls remained. The church was almost completely rebuilt and was re-dedicated in 1952. The two most outstanding features of the church are the beautiful stained-glass windows. The one over the west door depicts St George and the Dragon in all their splendour, and if one enters the church through this door a perfect reflection is made in the plain glass screen separating the bellchamber, which is the base of the tower, from the rest of the church. A second stained-glass window above the altar depicts the Ascension, with Christ in a glorious long, flowing, red robe. There are very few items of historic interest surviving, but of these, the brass plates dating from as far back as 1594 and the impressive reredos, reputed to have come from Italy many centuries ago, deserve mention.

We enjoyed the peace and tranquillity of these surroundings and felt that the remaining clear-glass windows, giving view to the countryside outside, enhanced this atmosphere.

Eventually we proceeded to the Rectory to meet the

Rev Denis Large. The Rectory is a typical old country mansion with rambling gardens and rooms too enormous to heat. The furnishings had been painstakingly chosen to harmonise with these surroundings. We were ushered into a large room which was refreshingly cool, despite the heat outside. A Press conference was about to take place. The reporters filed in silently and took their seats. There was a hush of anticipation as they waited to hear what it was all about. They were different people in this environment and were on their best behaviour.

The Rev Denis Large began by reading his prepared statement:

> To whoever was responsible for Genette's disappearance or to anyone else who might know what really took place on that Saturday afternoon.
>
> I do not want to know your name or where you are. I only want to end the terrible strain and distress which Genette's parents are suffering. Just tell me if Genette is still alive and give me some proof that she is. If she is dead, then tell me and, if you can, where her body may be found.
>
> Telephone me at my home, Clyst St George Rectory. I shall stay by the phone for twenty-four hours from noon Wednesday until noon on Thursday. If you telephone *I* shall answer. No one else will be listening. I promise that you will remain anonymous.

Afterwards he went on to explain that this was something that he was doing on his own initiative and that the police were not involved although, naturally, he had told them of his intentions and they fully understood his motives.

He was quite aware that he was likely to get some strange telephone calls and even crank calls, but he was willing to shoulder this burden in the hope that the person we had all been waiting to hear from would contact him.

We felt this was a fantastic idea. We were very concerned by the danger that the Rev Denis Large might be setting himself up as a target for everyone who might want to hit out at the Church and so on. We knew he would have hoax callers.

We left the Rectory and went home through the country lanes that connect Clyst St George and Aylesbeare. Normally we would have enjoyed this pretty country drive but now fate had given every clump of bushes, every hedgerow, a new twist, each in their turn became a possible hiding-place. The passengers in every car we passed were scrutinised in case Genette should be one of them. Each time we saw something white in the hedgerows or on the roadside, we stopped and examined it. Every journey we took was a nightmare of its own.

The following morning (Wednesday) we were preparing for Tania's return from Cornwall as the police were bringing her back on this particular day. We also decided to stay in to await any reaction that there might have been to the Vicar's twenty-four-hour telephone vigil, which was due to start at noon on that day.

During the morning we had a call from Mike Charleston of the *Daily Express*, to whom we gave our first exclusive press interview. He wanted to paint a pen-portrait of Genette. We went through various details together to enable him to write something a little bit different from what had been in the newspapers so far.

This was the first occasion that we had seen the gentler side of the press and we began to appreciate how helpful they could be to us. It was also the first occasion when anyone outside the family learned of Genette's nickname 'Ginny Boo'. We discussed Genette's personality, our fears, our hopes, and talked about how she had altered over the last months. The fact that she had been growing up — rather like that song 'Gigi'. The spark had come into her. We had had to stop calling her 'Boo' because she was becoming a young lady. But most of all we spoke about the one thing we all had in common — our love for 'Ginny Boo'.

At lunchtime Tania arrived home. Naturally there were tears, but she coped exceedingly well much to our relief — we had been very concerned before her return, not knowing quite how she was going to cope with it all.

Later in the afternoon we heard that the Vicar's vigil was going very well indeed. He was getting a lot of telephone calls but, unfortunately, a considerable number of them were hoax calls. We stayed up late that night as we felt almost obliged to keep him company, although we were some miles apart. It was well into the early hours of the morning when we finally went to bed, thinking very much about the sort of night he was probably having.

The following morning we switched on the radio to hear that he had worked through the night but that it had been a very tough experience for him. The phone had been going practically all night long. By the end of his vigil at midday, he had had many, many calls — most of them stupid, he felt. He also felt how incredible it was that so many people seemed to get pleasure out of just ringing his number and then hanging up. Lots of people said they could provide information and he advised them all to telephone the police. He heard from all sorts of weirdos, mystics and psychics, ranging from people who had had dreams to those who had seen UFOs. Some people had simply said that Genette was either alive or dead. Unfortunately the call he had been waiting for did not come.

Our hearts felt heavy as yet another hope began to fade, but, nevertheless, we felt relieved that this brave man's vigil had come to an end.

The hot sunshine continued and the corn turned more golden; the farmers began preparing to gather it in. Even after the wet summer we had endured the signs were there for a bumper yield. The combine harvesters were started up; the barns cleared out; spare tractors and trailers were made ready. But the usual happy harvest time in this area was going to take on a rather macabre twist. The plea went out from Detective Chief Superintendent Rundle for everyone to keep a watchful look out in front of the cutting blades of their machinery for any possible clues, or indeed Genette, as they worked around the fields, many of which had not yet been searched, apart from the air by helicopter. The fields of standing corn had been left, as naturally they did not want to destroy the crop unnecessarily, and one can normally see from the edge whether somebody has been into the field.

The police diving team had now searched over four hundred ponds, pools, ditches and wells in the area. A fairly formidable task, during which they had worked many hours in the most unbelievable places and under the most filthy conditions imaginable. In one instance we heard that they had come across an underground reservoir, its only access via a manhole, down which a diver descended. A diver had swum around in this dark underground cavern, the only light coming from the open manhole: he was certainly braver than I would have been and shivers went up my spine just thinking about it. We asked who he was but were immediately told that it was just part of his job.

During this same afternoon we heard that a stockbroker had added £1,000 to the reward fund, which had now reached £5,500. His reasons for offering the reward were, he said, that he had two daughters of his own and if a girl cannot be safe in a village like Aylesbeare, she cannot be safe anywhere in the world. This summed up very accurately the feelings of both of us and those of many others at this time. One expects this sort of thing in busy streets or on main roads, but never in a quiet, out-of-the-way by-lane.

Thursday had been a day of preparations in the village as everyone busied themselves making the church ready for the Flower Festival that was due to open on the Friday. This was the culmination of many months of careful flower growing. We had been asked several days previously if we wanted the Festival to go ahead. At the same time we were asked if the ringing of the church bells would upset us. My immediate reaction was, 'For goodness sake ring them. Genette might hear them and come home at their sound'. As to the Festival, how could we possibly deny people the beauty that this spectacle would provide — a taste of beauty that we all so desperately needed.

On the Friday morning we were given the opportunity to go and look at the Flower Festival prior to its official opening. No one particularly felt like meeting people but as Tania wanted to see the flowers I agreed to accompany her. As we approached the doorway we read the notice that had been pinned to the door: 'Spare a thought for Genette and her family whilst in this church'.

St Mary's Church, Aylesbeare, dates mostly from the fifteenth century, although the tower appears to have some thirteenth century masonry at the bottom and extensive repairs were carried out during the latter half of the nineteenth century. To our left, as we entered, the fourteenth century font had been colourfully decorated, with children in mind. The theme of the festival was 'Country Crafts': the kind of crafts which were everyday occupations in our village at one time. Some crafts had not only survived but gone from strength to strength, while others were enjoying a revival as hobbies.

Turning to the right at the font, past the List of Vicars, the first window illustrated carpentry, a craft without which the church and surrounding cottages would not have been built. The carpenter in the village used to live at Crossways Cottage. The next window along had cobbler's tools and shoes laid out to remind us of the boots and shoes that were once made in the cobbler's shop (now, the cottage known as Halls).

The pulpit was the next to have been splashed with colourful arrangements of flowers by another clever pair of hands. Behind the pulpit are some steps which at one time led to the rood loft (long since removed). The main altar with its rich colouring backed by its reredos from the now demolished St Edmund's Church, Exeter, had been made even more mellow, the orange and red theme depicting sunset. The side chapel windows depicted sunrise.

On the far side of the church the first window was adorned with loaves of bread, ornamental and otherwise, to illustrate the two bakeries that used to exist, one at the 'Blue Anchor' and the other at the Post Office. The next window along represented the main occupation in the village — farming. A little further along a spinning wheel depicted a craft that is enjoying a revival and we also saw here the various colours of wool obtained by using natural dyes from plants and berries. The back window reminded us of the craft with perhaps the most romantic associations, that of the village blacksmith, there having been two forges in the village, one at Truants and the other at 2 Bicton Cottages. The final window had been draped with the world-famous Honiton lace. This left two other crafts; that of cider making, at one time carried out on most farms; the other, corn dollies, the decorations traditionally made from the last stalks of corn in a field and kept safely until the seed was sown the following year.

As we wandered around we admired the beauty and colour so cleverly arranged by so many nimble fingers, yet even these were not nimble enough to form the delicate trumpets of the gladioli or paint these colours so adeptly. Who but God could provide us with such wonders?

I was yet again aware of the peace and tranquillity that are with me whenever I go into a church. I had noticed this before, many times — even in the centre of a very busy city. Outside can be humdrum, a lot of noise, cars going at high speed, here, there and everywhere; many people walking around — a continual din. Yet step inside the doors of a church and within a few moments — peace and quietness.

After we had spent this quiet hour around the church we made our way home to be greeted by the police. They had brought with them a note, which was the type of kidnap note that children write in play and the sort of thing that many people have put into a bottle at some time or another. They wanted to know whether or not it was Genette's handwriting. We went upstairs and got some of her school books to compare it with, although right from the beginning we were sure that it was not her writing. Eventually they took some samples away with them to send, complete with the kidnap note, to the handwriting specialists in Birmingham for them to compare scientifically.

Our store-cupboard was by now getting short of food. The winter before we had had quite a problem to last out the snow and had decided from that time onwards that we would always keep a reserve store and this had been well and truly depleted to the point where we had to face up to going out and doing some proper shopping. This was really to be quite a test for us. It would be the first time that we had faced people other than those involved in the search.

We set off in the car and went to our usual supermarket and started wheeling the basket around. It was a peculiar and unpleasant feeling. I don't know whether people did recognise us or not but one had the feeling that they did. We certainly felt they did. We wanted to be out of there as soon as possible, so we hurriedly did our shopping and went home.

On the two occasions when we were searching the woods Bob Cracknell had mentioned, we had noticed a wide stream running alongside the road for quite some distance. It had been nagging at our minds since then that it was a place which could so easily hide something pushed over the side and there it could stay hidden for a long time. In fact one could almost get a car over the side in places. So, that afternoon, we decided to go and walk the complete length of the ditch and stream alongside this road. The area we were looking at was within five miles of Aylesbeare to the back of Tipton St John (a nearby village). We drove to the spot where we had left the car on that Saturday a week or more ago. We put on our wellington boots, gathered together our rope, torch and sticks and clambered down over the bank. We were by this time well prepared for our search expeditions. On a previous occasion I had got into difficulties when, having gone over the side of an embankment, I had great difficulty in getting back up over the shale. From that moment on we carried a rope — just in case. We were often searching until after dark, and in some pretty dank and gloomy places during the day, so we always carried a torch with us.

At first the stream was about five foot wide with about four inches of water trickling along. The sides of the bank were very high above our heads. It was overgrown with brambles and thorns, but we slowly made our way downstream with the water babbling along in front of us, making its way easily through thick undergrowth which made our progress difficult.

We walked for a considerable distance, checking the banks on either side as we went, and in particular the bank on the roadside. At one moment we would be all hunched down with the brambles over our heads, and the next we would be out in the open as the stream widened, to meander round a bend.

After some distance, the stream gradually narrowed, then turned into a ditch and finally disappeared down a drainpipe. We felt satisfied that there was no point in going any further so we struggled back up the bank and returned along the road to the car. Yet again another search had drawn a blank.

The village during this weekend was very busy with people coming to the Flower Festival. The publicity surrounding Genette had drawn a tremendous amount of attention to Aylesbeare, the sort of attention this small community did not want. It was a sad village where people tried desperately to lead their normal lives, but everyone's thoughts were never far from Genette. Most people had had contact with her in one way or another. She sang in the village choir; she was also a Girl Guide and she daily took the dog for a walk and chatted to people she met along the way. Obviously these people were missing her almost as much as we were. Her friendly smile and her interest in what they were doing were no longer there.

Sunday was quite a big day. A Family Service, attended by the Right Reverend Wilfrid Westall, the former Bishop of Crediton, was held to celebrate the Flower Festival. It was one of the biggest congregations that I imagine Aylesbeare has ever seen. What a dreadful shame that something of this kind had to be the reason for people turning up in such large numbers to the church.

I went to church that morning with Tania. It needed considerable courage for both of us to walk down the aisle to the seat that had been specially kept for us. The churchwardens were not sure whether we would come or not and we ourselves had not decided until the last moment.

As we knelt, there was a mention of Genette in the prayers and the tears started to well in our eyes. I had to console Tania who was having difficulty in keeping her emotions under control, but she managed, and finally the service ended. As we came out the Rt Rev

Westall tried, like so many others, with kind words of comfort to express his sympathy.

On the path that led to home Tania was still a little weepy and I cheered her up by saying that things might not be so bad as they seem. 'Let's have hope.' And so we worked at getting our faith back. Always hoping and never giving up. Always looking on the positive side of things. There were still no facts, even now after all the questioning, after all the searching. Why should we presume that Genette was dead when there was not a single fact to suggest it?

Sunday was a day when I spent some considerable time in thought. Things seemed more desperate than they had before and I became even more depressed. I went up to look at Genette's empty bedroom to wonder, Where and Why? It was while I was feeling very low that the telephone rang. The call was from my employers asking me to go and see them the following day. This brought me back to reality with a bang and I was amazed to find that it was already 10.30 in the evening. I was vaguely aware that it had been a beautiful day outside, but the sun wasn't shining within our hearts.

3 The Search Widens

On Monday, 4 September, I got up and dressed and went off to see my employers. My return to work was a frustrating experience; I wanted to be in two places at once. Part of me knew I had to work, knew that I had to support my family: the other half of me desperately wanted to carry on searching, desperately wanted to be involved with everything going on. I began to be rather like a bear with a sore head. Underneath there was a seething anger that someone unknown had outrageously interfered with my hopes and dreams for my loved ones and myself. Many people who were friends of mine took the brunt of this pent-up emotion. Fortunately they understood. I was snappy, moody and apt to say things without thinking first. But then Genette was my only daughter and, due to the rare form of muscular dystrophy from which I had suffered since birth, would be my only daughter.

Some years ago when it was discovered that this disease was hereditary we had decided that, as I had one healthy child, I would not chance becoming a father again and possibly bringing into this world a serious invalid. I am hardly affected by the disease but many other people are less fortunate and suffer dreadfully as they gradually waste away, becoming more and more helpless as their life goes on. I couldn't in my heart help to bring into the world someone who would be unable to play sport, to run, walk or participate in an ordinary everyday life. I had been very fortunate in that

Genette had been found to have no trace of this disease. When my first marriage broke down it was because of all this that Genette was left in my care, Sheila not having the heart to part us. From that moment on Genette became ever more important.

In her I had seen a wonderful future. I had tried to mould her to see the things in life that were good and worthwhile. I endeavoured to tell her of my failings in the hope that she would not fall into the same pitfalls. I had taught her to have an interest in nature and to be kind and gentle to creatures great and small. With her had gone our hopes and dreams.

Wednesday morning, 6 September, brought reinforcements to the search parties when a hundred marines came to help comb more of the countryside at the back of Ottery St Mary, where thick fir plantations cover the steep hillsides that sweep up from the wide valley of the river Otter — the sort of area that is very hard to search and can only be successfully covered on foot.

On the following day (Thursday) the police issued the description of a teenager who had been seen on the verge of the main Exeter-Sidmouth road on the day that Genette had gone missing. They wanted to talk to this person and find out whether he had seen Genette or anything out of the ordinary. Within a few hours of putting out this appeal the teenager in question came forward and was eliminated from the enquiry.

During the evening a big meeting was held in the school. The police advised us to stay at home as they felt people would be less inhibited with us absent. Normally such a meeting would take place in the Village Hall, but this had been taken over by the police as their Incident Centre. Mr Christopher Shand, who is a herdsman in the village, with young children himself, decided to hold this public meeting to raise the reward fund and see if there was anything else that the villagers of Aylesbeare could do. People came to the meeting from Exeter, Exmouth, Tipton St John and Cullompton to try and help. Many questions were asked of the police who were in attendance there. Had the maroon car been eliminated? No. Had the drinkers at the White Horse been traced? Yes. Could the maroon vehicle have been a hire car? Possibly. Had all the car owners who passed through the village that afternoon been contacted? It was doubtful that they would ever find all of them. Had the Exe estuary been searched? Some parts of it. Would it be of any benefit to do another search of the immediate area, close to where Genette went missing? The area had been searched at least four times and on the fourth occasion very thoroughly, using the most modern techniques available. Discussion then turned to the reward fund. After much debate as to the wording of the terms of the reward, three options were put to the body of the meeting:

1 Safe return
2 Whereabouts
3 Evidence that she was alive and well.

A show of hands was asked for and the majority were in favour of 'Safe return'.

Someone said that if they were going to offer a bribe for someone to come forward with evidence, then in this day and age it would have to be a big one. A figure of £50,000 was mentioned and it was decided to make this the target. And so the appeal fund was launched. A team of volunteers led by Chris and Diana Shand addressed many envelopes to send out to major employers and large commercial firms throughout East Devon enclosing the following letter:

September 1978

Dear Sir,

Genette TATE

You are no doubt aware of the disappearance of 13-year-old Genette Tate from our village under mysterious circumstances on Saturday, 19 August. Despite many police enquiries and organised searches of the surrounding countryside there is no clue as to Genette's present whereabouts.

At a well attended meeting of villagers on 7th instant a resolution was carried that we seek assistance from business concerns in the East Devon area in an effort, if possible, to raise the reward, which was kindly started by the Express and Echo newspaper, to £50,000.

What we have in mind is that organisations or persons wishing to be associated with the venture contact the newspaper offices at Sidwell Street, Exeter (Tel. No. Exeter 73051) direct with a pledge of a set sum; on the other hand, I should be happy to accept such a pledge on your behalf for onward transmission.

I emphasise that the reward will only be paid to a person providing information leading to Genette's safe return. The police have been consulted on this issue and are happy with the above arrangement.

It is difficult to convey to you the feeling of despair we all have and hope that you can join us in our efforts to bring about a happy conclusion.

Yours faithfully,

CHRISTOPHER SHAND

By Saturday evening the fund had reached £10,000.

Yet another big search was organised. An appeal went out on Saturday evening for people to help the East Devon Deer Control Society search East Hill Strips from the back of Ottery St Mary along the steep wooded ridge that runs towards Sidmouth. This was to take place on Sunday, 10 September. As many volunteers as possible were needed so that a thorough search could be organised with people going shoulder to shoulder through the dense plantations. There were going to be two helicopters involved as well. On the Sunday afternoon some friends arrived to help in the search; but because of the nature of the terrain it was decided that it would be absolutely useless for me to go.

The day before we had been talking to a psychic who had given us a description of a picture she had in her mind of a stream that was too wide to jump, on the far side of which were evergreen trees and just to the edge of the picture a man-made construction that was either a boat, a fence, or something similar. We studied the ordnance survey map and picked out all the areas where coniferous woods were shown and where the ground was reasonably flat, with a river or stream nearby. While the Deer Control Society's search was on Vi and I set off with the dog to go and check out some of these locations. We drove along many country lanes that afternoon, checking first one spot and then another. Where we couldn't drive we walked, covering quite a few fields. Eventually we grew tired and it started to rain so we returned to Aylesbeare.

Shortly after this the East Hill searchers returned home. Tania and Sheila had taken part and also several other friends of ours. We listened to them describing the walking conditions. They had been formed into lines, close enough to touch one another, and then moved off slowly through the forest a pace at a time. Whenever anything unusual was found the whole line was stopped until the object had been investigated and then the line moved on again. The amazing thing was that, although people were almost shoulder to shoulder, there were places where the trees and undergrowth were so dense that you could not see the person next to you. Progress was slow in the high bracken and painful through the prickly gorse bushes. Tania and Sheila returned home covered in scratches. They were worn out and their legs were aching. I was very glad that I had not attempted this arduous task.

We felt a lot better after this search because it covered part of the wooded area that Bob Cracknell had been talking about and we were relieved to know that this area could be mostly eliminated from the enquiry. In fact by Tuesday 12 September the police with the marines had eliminated East Hill Strips completely. Also by that Tuesday the divers had completed their work and the number of detectives working on the case was reduced to a hundred. These men had been borrowed from all over Devon and some of them had to be returned. The information was not coming in quite so fast now.

The days were now beginning to return to some kind of normality, although many hours were spent discussing new ideas and new theories. The publicity had died down and people were beginning to forget. It wasn't until someone said to me that they had overheard a conversation in which it was mentioned that the 'little girl in Aylesbeare had been found' that we decided to try and put something about this into a newspaper. I phoned Mike Charleston of the *Daily Express* and told him that I would like to write my own headline and he agreed to see what could be done. That was on the evening of Sunday the 17th — on Monday morning our headline 'OUR LITTLE GIRL IS STILL MISSING' was in the paper together with a write-up. On the same day we were delighted to see the stickers that an insurance company, who wished to remain anonymous, had arranged to have printed. They had a picture of Genette on them with the words 'FIND GENETTE'. Many of these were distributed by police throughout the country.

Monday was also the day when the kidnap note we had been shown days earlier was released to the press. The handwriting experts had decided they could not eliminate it but could not be sure that it was Genette's writing. It was issued to the press in the morning. The first news of it came over the radio at lunchtime. Within an hour the girl who had written it telephoned Scotland Yard to say that she was responsible. Whilst on holiday in North Wales driving from one place to another she had become bored and had been doodling on a piece of paper. The wind took the paper out through the car window and some days later a pedestrian had picked it up and handed it in to the police. It was the type of thing that could happen to anyone. We were horrified to see the following day that some of the newspapers were condemning this little girl when in fact we felt she deserved praise for coming forward so quickly — many would just not have bothered. The police might have been involved in days of searching in the difficult terrain of the Welsh mountains where the note was found, if she had not acted so quickly and responsibly.

On the Wednesday at the regular press conference, the police announced that they were launching the hunt for Genette on a national scale as the local searches had proved unsuccessful. They started distributing posters describing Genette to every police station in the country.

Later in the day we were asked to go down to the BBC Studios in Plymouth to appear with the police on 'Nationwide' to launch a national TV appeal for information about Genette. This was a most unnerving experience. We — Violet, Detective Chief Superintendent Rundle and myself — sat in comfortable chairs upon a dais. The studio crew pinned microphones on to our clothing and tried to put us at ease. The heat under the spot lamps was unbearable. We watched with interest the part of the programme that preceded us and then came our turn.

The interviewer's voice came to us through a loudspeaker placed behind us — he was in London and we were in Plymouth. You couldn't see who you were talking to and at the same time we didn't know that we were being spoken to until the camera pointed at us. It was difficult to say the least and needed a great deal of concentration. We were glad when it was over and went to collect Tania from the viewing lounge where she had been watching the programme. Outside in the cool, fresh air again, we decided to stay in Plymouth for a meal. This was the first time we had dined out since Genette had gone missing.

On Saturday, 23 September, we decided to do something ourselves about distributing the car stickers. We collected a bundle of five hundred or so from the police and went to the Exeter motorway services area at the end of the M5. We waved down the cars as they were leaving and gave them a sticker to put on their back windows. It was a very hot day and it was a tiring and arduous occupation.

Violet went back to work on the Sunday. We dropped her off at the hospital at 8am before Tania, her boyfriend and myself returned to the Exeter services area to continue our sticker distribution. We parked the car so that it was sideways on to the oncoming cars and stuck large posters of Genette on its side. We also erected another board bearing the words: 'If you are going out of this area, we need your help'. We then set about waving the cars down; at times we had as many as five cars lined up, putting the stickers on their back windows. From here cars were going all over the country and we were very pleased when someone pulled in to say that they were going to the north of Scotland. By the end of the morning, when we had to collect Vi from the hospital after her shift, we had distributed over a thousand leaflets since we had started.

That Sunday an article appeared in the *Observer* which upset us by inferring that Genette was dead. This was not the only article to make such a suggestion, and, although we accepted the terrible possibility, we were always very hurt and annoyed because we felt that people could all too easily take it to be fact. After all there were no clues or definite facts to suggest that she was dead, and the suggestion alone might make it harder for us to get the public's co-operation.

Early on the Wednesday morning Violet and I were wandering over the fields close to the spot where Genette had last been seen, trying to work out for ourselves how far a car could have driven off the road and into the fields, and whether it would have been hidden from the road, when we came upon some burn marks in the grass, sweeping out in a large curve. We looked around and found further round blotches, also obviously burn marks, and in the centre of one of these was a pile of white crystals. We went to the police station and told them of our findings, to be greeted with the news that yet another search of this area was due to start that very morning following information received from a Dutch medium. I left them to it and went off to work.

The burn marks were later to attract interest from UFO investigators — I will return to them later. I was to discover that the police will follow up a lead given to them by a reputable psychic but will not entertain UFOlogists for a moment. The police used publicity most effectively to keep Genette's case in the public eye, and it was partly for this reason that so much of the psychic's work received such wide press coverage. But any suggestion of a UFO met with a deaf ear and they tried to play down as much as possible the fact that the *Express and Echo* which Genette was delivering when she disappeared had carried a story and picture of a UFO over Exeter.

The reward was gradually creeping up and by the following day (Thursday) it had reached £20,000. It was decided that, in order to prevent someone from holding Genette in the hope that the reward would go even higher, the reward fund should be closed on Saturday, 30 September.

On Friday a new search, instigated by a medium, took place at Castle Drogo, near Drewsteignton, on a large estate administered by the National Trust. The Dartmoor Rescue Team helped on this one and within a few hours they had eliminated this area.

Saturday the 30th came and the reward fund closed at £23,056. The following day a problem that we had been concerned about from the beginning was highlighted by the press: which photograph of Genette was the best likeness? School photographs are not taken at regular intervals, and the particular photograph, showing Genette with short hair, that was used for the posters and handbills was taken when Genette was at school in Gorran Haven three years previously, The prime reason for using this photograph was that she had taken it to the hairdresser only a few weeks before to enable him to copy the exact style of her hair and hence it bore the greatest resemblance to her hairstyle when she disappeared. The other photograph that had been circulated, particularly by the *Daily Mirror* on its posters, showed Genette with longer hair. Although the *Mirror* picture was more recent and had been taken during her first year at Exmouth School when she was eleven years old, it was misleading because of the longer hair style. The school photograph also was not as up to date as I felt it might have been. We had snapshots which were much more recent, but all of them showed her just before she had had her hair cut and when they were blown up to any size they became hazy and blurred and totally useless as far as posters were concerned. The Press made the point, a sensible one in my view, that photographs should be taken, professionally, and annually, of all school children. We feel that schools should keep a photographic record, so that, in the event of a child going missing, the police can quickly obtain a recent photograph.

As the days went by we continually received many letters from people in all parts of the country and from all walks of life. Many of them were extending their enormous sympathy. We had letters from friends who did not know quite what to write and letters from well-meaning people with their own particular theories. Some of these were rather strange and some were straightforward, containing good ideas. All those that contained theories or suggestions were passed on to the police to be perused and followed up.

One particular letter contained a newspaper cutting and written all round this cutting were a lot of words containing clues, for example: 'Go past a monument or gateway similar to Marble Arch'. 'Look in the blackberry bushes near a house.' From the jottings that came with the letter it appeared that this person got inspiration from listening to peculiar music!

We also received requests for many different things: a piece of Genette's hair; some of her clothing (some of them wanted clothing that had been unwashed); a drawing that she had done; or any little article that she had cherished. When we felt we were dealing with someone who was intelligent and might have something to offer, we complied with their request.

Naturally we had letters with prayers in them. We had one in particular which came with a picture of Jalaram Bapa, an Indian guru, with instructions to place the picture near a candle which should be lit and kept burning for twenty-four hours, during which time one had to pray continuously, and then the answer would be forthcoming. Some people just wrote and gave us the names of mediums or seers to contact.

Altogether we and the police received nearly seven hundred different theories, either by post, telephone or by word of mouth. Our attitude was the same with everyone who approached us personally. We would sit down and listen to them with a completely open mind. Our feeling was that one of them just might hold the solution to the problem. We were dealing with so many people that it became more and more probable, by the law of averages, that the correct solution had been presented to us — but which one?

During this time many people called at our house. On one occasion an old lady arrived, complete with wicker table, sat down in a corner of the room and called up her 'spirit guide' — a Red Indian Chief named 'Golden Dawn'. She set about communicating with this spirit by repeating over and over again the letters of the alphabet, leaving one letter out each time so that the word she was getting from the spirit would be gradually made up. Obviously it was a long-drawn-out affair. We started at about 7 o'clock in the evening and this dear old lady was still going strong two-and-a-half hours later. She told us that two young men had been involved in snatching Genette. They had not bribed her with sweets or anything; they had just grabbed her, laughing all the time, bundled her into the back of a grey van that had had a recent tyre change — the spirit insisted that the police should check all the tyres in the area. They had then taken her out of the search area until their house had been checked, but now she had been brought back.

We asked where Genette was and were told that she was five miles in the direction that the birds fly when they migrate, and that nearby was a church with a saint on the window. We asked whether Genette could hear anything and were told that she could hear the sound of running water and light traffic. We were also told that she could not see out of the window of the room she was in. We were told to go back to 'number five well', whatever that was. The spirit assured us that she wasn't in the well but nearby. When asked if she was all right, he said that she was alive but was not very well. She had had some problem with her throat and suggested that we check all the chemists to see if anyone had been in to try to get something for a throat condition.

All the time there was a great deal of urgency. 'Go now', he said, 'urgent'. We were also told to bear in mind the number five because it had great relevance. 'To keep thinking of number fives and the answer would eventually come 1-2-3-4 ...'

It is difficult to know whether to take this sort of thing seriously, at the time we were prepared to try anything, but now, nearly a year later, we are a lot more sceptical.

When the lady left, although it was late in the evening, we immediately went to the police and told them all that had happened. We also drove to a nearby village, where the spirit guide had said we would find the place where Genette was being held, and looked around for the grey van, but we did not find one. We also stopped and talked to various people about possible wells in the village.

Thinking back on it, I imagine we must have caused quite a stir; wandering about the village after dark at around 10pm and asking about deep wells!

Another clue involved two words — 'Oasis Pond', which we were assured would link up with the name of the house where Genette was held. We had already established from the local policeman that there was no house of this name or even one with the word 'Oasis' as part of its name. I scoured the village again the following night after work looking for houses with names even vaguely similar to 'Oasis'. We mentioned it to other people because we felt the more minds we could get concentrating on it, the greater the chance of coming up with something.

Our hopes were raised quite a bit by the old woman's visit, but we were, of course, clutching at straws and believed practically anything. Later the memory of this episode was like a black comedy, but not at the time.

On Wednesday, 4 October, two special police dogs arrived in the village. They had been used for finding dead Israelis and Egyptians buried on the battlefields of the Middle East. They were brought in to search a field within a mile of Aylesbeare on the basis of information given to the police by a top European psychic. The dogs spent quite some time going over this field. I felt it was a complete waste of time because I was so convinced that Genette was alive, and I said so — as I have on many occasions when asked for my thoughts on this. However, the dogs did locate a number of possible graves and the police started to dig these up. For two days they continued digging in the middle of this ploughed field.

I thought at the time how thankless a task this was — a bit macabre too, not knowing what might be found. By all accounts the dogs had been trained to find any kind of rotting meat so that if there was a bird, rabbit or any animal buried, they would find it. After a lot of digging all that the dogs actually found were the remains of several small animals. Nevertheless, it was a horrible feeling returning to the village from work each day and seeing the police still working; despite our very strong conviction that Genette was still alive.

It was very hard to hold on to this belief with that kind of activity going on around us. Inwardly, a constant battle was being waged; every now and again we would doubt the certainty that she was alive and allowed negative thoughts to creep in: 'Perhaps she's dead ... Perhaps she's out there ... Oh, God I hope not!' Our relief when the police had finished this particular task was immense.

At about this time the *Daily Express* printed the most recent snapshot, taken by a friend, that we possessed of Genette. Of course, when this friend had clicked the shutter she could not have thought that it would ever appear on the front page of a national newspaper.

And so the bright days of summer turned into hazy autumn gold. The hedgerows became much easier to search and we spent many hours going along various roadsides in the area. The woods with their new ankle-deep covering of fallen yellow and bronze leaves became virtually impossible to search. But our quest continued.

We made plans for our own telephone vigil and on 13 October the GPO installed a special number for us. I issued a press release and sent it by post to various newspapers and also delivered it by hand to some of the local ones. It read:

> Over the last weeks my wife and I have listened to many theories from many people. All have been painstakingly followed up — to no avail and we are left with nothing positive enough to bring about a

solution to the problem of Genette's disappearance.

We are both convinced she is still alive — possibly held somewhere against her will. There must be somebody who is aware of the true facts and is perhaps too frightened to come forward. It is for this reason that I am making myself accessible by telephone to anyone who genuinely wishes to contact me direct, and possibly anonymously, in order to pass on some hard facts that will lead to a solution to the mystery.

All calls will, of course, be treated in strictest confidence.

From midday on Saturday, 14th October, to midday on Sunday, 15th October, I shall personally answer the telephone.

We would like to remind everyone of the reward which is a little in excess of £23,000 and is payable for information leading directly to the safe return of Genette.

Unfortunately the press did not give this release the national coverage we desperately needed; it was one of the few times that we did not get their co-operation. We had excellent coverage in the local newspapers and on local radio but only one national newspaper, *The Times*, published the statement and they misprinted the telephone number!

We had a lot of phone calls over the weekend. At 2 o'clock on Saturday morning I was awakened by the phone ringing. My heart was thumping inside my chest as though it was trying to escape. I reached out in the darkness to my bedside telephone, afraid of who might be on the other end. What a relief when a dear old lady, suffering from insomnia, began chatting about all that she had read in the newspapers. After our conversation finished I went back to sleep hoping that she would also.

At about 10am the calls started to come in one after another. Generally they were from people offering help: mediums, psychics, people claiming extra-sensory powers, and so on. No one had any precise information to offer — no actual clues to give us. During the afternoon I was pestered every half hour by a man who insisted that Genette was in a caravan on the main Sidmouth Road. He had been in touch with the police and they were checking it out, but each time he rang he was becoming more and more impatient. I was later to learn that this man had obtained his information by swinging a pendulum alternately over his Jack Russell terrier and an ordnance survey map of the area! When he had narrowed down the area in this way, he paid a visit to the locality and found a locked caravan. He was convinced that Genette would be found inside.

Another call came from someone who said that Genette had been to her front window that very morning and tapped on the pane. She had recognised her by her T-shirt and gave a very vivid description of how muddy and bedraggled she had been — even to the extent of bleeding from a wound. When she approached the window and opened it Genette ran away along the garden path. This was promptly investigated by the police and found to be a complete figment of her imagination.

I continued to wait by the telephone. At times I was answering one call after another, grabbing a cup of soup or a hot drink in between, then back to the telephone, taking notes and passing on information to the police.

On Saturday night I slept on the settee by the side of the telephone in case of a call during the night. The last one came through at about half past eleven and from then on it was peace. I slept right through until the following morning and it was not until about noon on Sunday that the telephone first rang again. The calls continued after midday and into the late afternoon; but eventually they tapered off.

On Monday morning we had an influx of post; obviously from people who felt they would write rather than ring. Amongst the letters was one giving a location from a pendulum dowser who felt that Genette was around the Christchurch Playing Fields side of Reading. He had obtained this information by using an old RAC book and he felt that a car might have been locked up somewhere and a river launch or boat used as transport from that point onwards. He continued by pointing out that one can go a long way these days by rivers and canals.

Another letter was from a gentleman who has continually sent us snapshots of various views throughout Devon. Sometimes it would be a picture of Exmouth in the summertime or a view across Whipton, Exeter, and on one occasion we had a picture of a couple of goats browsing in a hedge! We never did quite figure out what this was all about, but all were conscientiously passed on to the police for examination.

We also had several offers from people to do a horoscope of Genette's life. They wanted us to provide them with her date and time of birth and, in return, they would send us the horoscope. Very few just sent back a straight horoscope; the majority could not resist the temptation of including their own thoughts and theories as well.

One of the strangest letters we received was from someone suggesting that a chair be taken and placed where the bicycle and newspapers had been abandoned and that I should sit on it for a few minutes every day; the hope being that word would get around that I was doing this and that perhaps the person who had taken Genette would come back to have a look at me, to see what I looked like! I never did get up the nerve to do this, thinking it rather eccentric.

The theories continued to come in. The callers continued to call.

A dowser came to the house with his pendulum. In order to carry out his ritual he needed some article that was very personal to Genette. He said that either blood or saliva gave the best results — we could provide neither. He experimented with various things: Genette's toy panda, her pack of playing cards, allowing his perfectly shaped resin pendulum to swing in various directions over each object in turn and then alternately over her photograph. Eventually he settled for her spectacle case and one of her unwashed socks. He took these articles with him and set off for the Police Incident Centre, where he shut himself away and busied himself with his maps and things. He came up with several locations which the police duly checked out, but nothing was found.

While he was working we had tried to find out how his pendulum worked. He had told us when he was in the house that we didn't have to use any special pendulum — even a wedding ring suspended from a piece of fine thread would do. I threaded up my ring and we found that we could get it to rotate — at least

Tania and I could, but Violet wasn't so successful and thought we were doing something to make it happen. Sometimes the ring would go round in circles and sometimes to and fro. On his return to the house we enquired further and tried to get him to explain what the different movements actually meant, but he seemed reluctant to part with his trade secrets and we continue to wonder just what, if anything, is the significance of the different movements of the pendulum and what makes them occur. The only conclusion I came to at the time was that the ordnance survey maps seemed full of strange powers, considering they are just sheets of paper with pretty patterns all over them, but I am still fascinated to see my ring spinning round in wide circles at high speed on the end of a piece of thread.

On Sunday, 22 October, an arrangement was made by a national newspaper to bring us together with another couple who were in the same situation as ourselves.

Mark Berkshire, who unfortunately was some time later found dead, had been missing for thirty days. Genette had now been missing for sixty-seven days. The *Daily Mirror* brought Pat Berkshire and her husband, Brian, to see us in Devon. Our day-to-day lives were worlds apart — Pat came from South London, whereas we were both country-born and bred — but we were drawn together by a bond of grief and found a tremendous amount of comfort in each other's company. For the first time we really felt that someone knew what they were saying when they said to us: 'We know how you must feel'. Just a short sentence but one that came from the heart. The plan was to have just a quick cup of tea and a short chat, then a photograph or two and they would be away. In fact we spent the entire afternoon talking and comparing their experiences in London with ours in Devon. From our conversation grew the original seed of the idea for 'International Find a Child'.

Although police methods were good in both places, some aspects were better in one area than in the other. For example, our police public relations office here had been very good. They had organised police press conferences, where we were taken along to meet all the press in one go. In Pat's case she had had journalists knocking at the door continuously. We realized that we had received a tremendous amount of coverage in the press and on television in comparison to the meagre amount that Pat had received.

The circumstances surrounding Mark's disappearance were just as mysterious as those concerning Genette. They had just as little idea of where Mark was as we had of where Genette was. In stark contrast, only two clairvoyants had offered to help Pat and only one medium wrote to her; but thank goodness, none of us had received any hoax calls.

Some one hundred and fifty photographs were taken of us during that afternoon but only one was published, with the article in the *Daily Mirror* on Wednesday, 25 October.

It was during this week that the police left Aylesbeare. They closed their temporary Incident Centre and ended what was for them a long, weary and fruitless enquiry. We felt very sad at their going but we knew in our hearts that the village had to get back to some kind of normality and the villagers needed the Village Hall for themselves. As I drove round the corner and into the village at lunchtime that day to talk to the television people, who had come to make a film of the mass exodus, it was with a feeling of sadness that I realised that no longer would I be making my daily trek to the Village Hall to find out if there was any news and that the friendly faces of the policemen, who had become my friends, would be gone.

The television people were already at home waiting for me when I arrived back. We went out into the garden to talk. They asked us how we felt now that the police had left. We told them that although the police were leaving, our hopes would not diminish. We still felt very definitely that Genette would be found alive. We knew that the police were continuing the investigation with a team of twenty detectives and that they had not given up hope. Local enquiries had largely petered out and they were dealing with enquiries at a much more national level, so it made more sense for them to be based at Exeter. We agreed we were disappointed that no solution had been found. We were also angry that someone somewhere knew the answer but was keeping quiet.

When the police moved out of the Village Hall they took with them hundreds of boxes containing 2,300 statements, 3,000 questionnaires and 3,200 enquiry forms. The last thing to go was Genette's bicycle, which we felt very sad about. All they left behind was a poster bearing a large picture of Genette.

The same day we heard that the BBC's 'Tonight' team were to show their programme on hypnosis. The title they had given it was: 'Where is Genette Now?'.

We got a friend to print out on some small pieces of paper: 'Where is Genette Now? Watch BBC1 tonight 11.10pm' and then busily circulated them to every single house in the village. We wanted as many people in the area as possible to watch the television, in the hope that, while watching the programme, it would trigger off something in their minds and they would remember some forgotten detail from that day.

The 'Tonight' team had, with the consent of the police, hypnotised two witnesses — Mrs Mathilda Rogers and her daughter, Gail. Under hypnosis they had obtained a more comprehensive description of the car that the police had been trying to trace. It was now said to be a maroon Triumph saloon, probably a 1300. They also constructed, with the help of an artist, a portrait of the driver of this car. Under hypnosis the letters of the registration number were also revealed, although not all of them. It was possibly 'MB' or 'BM' followed by another letter and then followed by the numbers which had a figure '1' amongst them and the suffix 'G'. All the possible computations of these letters and numbers were fed through the national vehicle computer in Swansea and it came back with about forty possibilities, which the police immediately set about checking.

The information obtained under hypnosis was very complete, even to the extent of a detailed description of the interior of the car, the fact that the radio was on, the colour of the man's eyes and so on. We hoped that from this something worthwhile would come.

Hypnosis is used in police questioning in many countries of the world, and in particular the United States. It has produced some very useful evidence where previously very little had existed. So far there has not been a case in this country in which hypnosis has proved to be of any value to the police and their attitude was summed up very clearly when they issued a statement saying: 'We have no means of knowing whether or not the information given under hypnosis is correct. However, we understand that statements given under hypnosis are reasonably reliable, but the task is by no means as easy as television viewers may believe.'

They also stated that they were not thinking of having other witnesses hypnotised. We felt this was a mistake because we thought it might bring to light other aspects of the case, in particular from the two girls who had last seen Genette. Under hypnosis they might have remembered something more — perhaps some information that had been blotted out of their minds for one reason or another. We felt that it would be a logical second step following the first hypnosis experiment.

On the following day (Friday) Pat Berkshire succeeded in getting a forty-second, peak viewing-time spot on television. She had put a lot of hard work into achieving this.

Most national newspapers by now were carrying a story about the hypnosis session, including comparisons of the police identikit picture with the oil painting of the wanted young man.

The village returned to a state of peace, but not peace of mind. The swings in the playground still stood idle. Mothers still accompanied their children to and from school and panicked when a child took longer than it should on an errand. Every man in the village still acted as a detective and took the registration number of any strange vehicle and eyed every stranger with suspicion. The police still came to check out this little point or that little point. But gone were the regular daily meetings of all the police involved in the case.

At about 9 o'clock each morning the police would go off in their cars to various parts of the country, and just before 9 o'clock in the evening there would be the rush of vehicles returning to the hall to report their findings, having completed their individual enquiries.) The telephones, that at times had rung continuously for twenty-four hours, had been taken away from the Village Hall. The local women who had cooked meals day after day, brewed tea and made sandwiches for the men searching for Genette had packed up. And the big brown canvas marquee erected next to the Hall and the special radio mast was removed. Also gone were the two police caravans from their spot behind the Hall.

Left behind were blackened patches in the grass as if a fun fair had moved on, and a broken grass bank where people had gone up and over the bank instead of up the steps and along the path, little trackways through the grass made by feet continuously passing to and fro, and an emptiness throughout the entire village — still waiting for news, for news of Genette.

4   UFOs

On Sunday, 29 October, British Summertime officially ended. It was frustrating to sit through the long winter evenings after I returned home from work. The only time when we could do any real searching or anything else out in the open was at weekends. Our seven-day week had suddenly been reduced to a two-day week.

A strange night-time happening began on Friday, 3 November, when a young man arrived at the door before I returned home from work and told Violet that he was going to bring Genette back. He was fairly certain that she would be returned either that night or the following one. Naturally she invited him in with open arms and by the time I arrived home he had told her all about his predictions. He was a very unusual man, but we treated him, like everyone else, with a completely open mind and sat and listened to what he had to say. After all, one is curious to understand motives, if nothing else.

He said he was the reincarnation of a 5,000-year-old Eastern god. He also claimed to be a guru. He said he had been praying and had called upon 'the Nazarene' to return to this earth now and put to rights the awful mess that the world was in. He had also worked out by numerology that Genette would be returned home early in the morning of either 4 or 5 November. As I understood it, because she had been taken at 3.33pm, he had estimated that she would be returned at 3.33am. We asked him where Genette was and he insisted that she had been taken by Venusians who, according to him, live in a spirit form around the planet Venus and not actually on it. He also said that her return should be kept a secret, and that it would be necessary to keep people away from the area because it had been noticed in the past that when UFOs appeared, people suffered burns or contracted cancer and some had also lost their sight. He said that Genette's return would be associated with a good deal of UFO activity. He also spoke of the possibility of a sacrificial exchange being demanded by the Venusians and was quite prepared to offer himself in exchange for Genette. We asked him why he wasn't afraid of being killed and he told us that, because he was a reincarnated god, he was immortal, and went on to give us several examples of how he had survived experiences that would have finished off mere mortals like us.

We listened with an unreal fascination to his theories about UFOs and reincarnation. He asked us if there were any unusual burn marks in the area near to where Genette had disappeared. Were there any electrical problems the night she went? Amazingly enough we could provide him with ample evidence of both. Yes, there were burn marks in a nearby field but we were pretty certain they had been caused by a chemical fertiliser, although we weren't sure. Yes, there had been an electrical fault that night. We had had a power cut — not for very long, just a short interruption to the supply. (We learned later that this had been caused by a fire in a nearby electrical sub-station on the same evening, although the end of the power line was in the same field as the burn marks.) Also there had been the UFO story and picture in the very paper Genette had been delivering. We began to regard this young man a little less sceptically.

He also fitted the description of the man the police were wanting to interview. He was about thirty years old, rather handsome with a good suntan, black hair and blue eyes, and although he was British he had a distinctly Asian appearance.

It occurred to us that his story might be a ruse to enable him to return Genette without any witnesses present. His plan was to carry out an all-night vigil at the spot where Genette had disappeared, his theory being that she would be beamed down to the same place that she had been beamed up from. After he had disclosed his theory to us he went home to get some warmer clothes, having arranged to return at about midnight. As soon as he had gone we telephoned the police to tell them of our suspicions.

Tania had arranged to go to a disco dance that evening with her boyfriend so Violet and I gave them a lift before going on into Exeter, where I took Vi for a meal at her favourite place, 'The Ship' — this was as an early surprise for her birthday the following day.

On our return journey we collected Tania and David from the disco, dropped David at his home and then drove home via Within Lane.

We found that we now used this route frequently, whereas prior to Genette's disappearance it had been an almost unknown road to us. Now I knew every inch of it: every bit of hedgerow and the exact location of every piece of rubbish. If anything new appeared we would stop and examine it, always hopeful that here might be the clue that we so desperately longed for. I suppose in our hearts we secretly hoped that by continually driving along this lane, one day Genette would be there, just waiting at that spot. The three hundred yards from where Tracey and Margaret had last seen her to where the bicycle was later found, we had searched many times, going over much of it on our hands and knees. If only we had found a two-pence piece it would have been some consolation, but nothing was found.

Shortly after returning home the young 'guru' was back. He parked his car and collected Genette's favourite 'Panda' teddy bear so that he would have something she would recognise, and off he went to start his vigil. We put on some warm clothes after he had gone and followed him secretly to see what he was up to. It was all very creepy. Vi and Tania were both hanging on to me very tightly as we made our way by moonlight through the village. We were so tense that the slightest noise or movement took on a sinister meaning. We did not know quite what to expect. The sky was clear with not a cloud in sight and all around the stars were twinkling brightly. We continued along Within Lane to within fifty yards of the spot where Genette had disappeared. There he sat on the ground with a blanket wrapped round him in a relaxed yoga position.

Then the most amazing thing happened. Great big flashing lights appeared over the horizon. We thought, 'My God — this is it!' They were coming at some speed down the hill into the village. Our hearts stood still and we clung to each other in anticipation. We really thought that Genette was being returned to us. In reality however it turned out to be only a police car which had come to check our young friend out.

After the police had satisfied themselves that the young guru was harmless they went on their way leaving us to wait for the expected UFO.

Our eyes and minds were very alert as we gazed skywards. Every glimmer of light or twinkling star caused us to look a second time. Even the light from the telephone box across the field which flickered through the leaves of a bush caused a good deal of discussion about its possible source. 3.33am came and went and at about 4 o'clock in the morning the young man went home, promising to return the following day.

The next day was Violet's birthday and she had invited her friend, Nanette, for the day. During the afternoon a photographer arrived to take some shots of us searching on some nearby moorland. We felt terrible doing this; it seemed so false — pretending to search.

On our return home we met the young guru who had come to look at the burn marks in the field. I took him across the field and showed him the lines. His excitement was unbelievable. We wandered around for quite some time and then returned to the house for tea. We sat and discussed many things with him until it was time for him to begin his second vigil.

It had been my intention to accompany him, but I fell asleep in a chair. The next thing I knew it was daylight — I had slept right through. He had gone home and that was that.

At about this time stories of black magic rituals that had supposedly taken place in Aylesbeare began to appear in the newspapers. It all started from a conversation overheard in a public house which was reported to have taken place between two detectives. One had told the other to lower his voice after they had started discussing evidence of black magic that they had found and how scared they had been.

Naturally, the police were asked to comment on this allegation but they insisted that they had found nothing in the village to suggest anything of the kind and added that, in a close-knit community like Aylesbeare, the idea was inconceivable. And there the story ended.

The next two weeks of November passed by with very little of any consequence occurring. But at the end of the month the Dutch medium, Mr Croiset, came up with more information which resulted in a renewed search of the river Clyst and the return of the police frogmen. They concentrated on the sluice gates before searching a complete three-mile stretch of the river without finding any clues.

While this was going on those horrible shivers returned once again. We hoped and prayed that they would not find Genette, particularly there, as she had always had a dislike of water.

We gathered that the Dutchman had had considerable success in previous enquiries throughout the world, but his theories made little impression on us because our belief that Genette was still alive was unshakeable.

On Saturday 25 November, Pat Berkshire's little boy, Mark, was found. Her waiting had ended in horror. His body was discovered in a churchyard, within one mile of his home, two months to the day after he had vanished. A dog, in fact, discovered the body and the death was now being treated as a case of murder. The news came like a cold hand gripping at my heart. We felt so sad, so sorry that this had to be the terrible ending to his mother's hope. Also, naturally, it made us wonder whether the police might not have missed something near Aylesbeare, although we didn't think so, having seen them at work and having done so much searching ourselves.

We tried desperately to contact Mark's parents to give them our sympathy and understanding; only eventually did we manage to get a message to them via the *Daily Mirror*. We couldn't really think of what to say apart from the fact that we were thinking of them and how sorry we were. We knew that for us the waiting must go on.

That weekend was a terrible time. We became more and more annoyed as every radio broadcast gave details of Mark's death — his poor mother had struggled so hard to get publicity when he first went missing. How many times had it been on the radio then? Yet now every half-hour the news of his death was being broadcast and we felt very bitter. We also felt angry and bemused by the fact that Mark's body had not been found before, for it was so close to home. How had they missed it? How was it possible to miss it?

On the Monday I had a day off work so I took the dog for a walk on Dartmoor to get away. I wanted to clear my mind and get away from everybody for a while. I walked up to a very high point, through an ancient Bronze Age village. The dog enjoyed herself sniffing at rabbit holes and I enjoyed a morning of peace. I returned home, collecting Vi on the way.

On Tuesday 28 November the psychic research team moved into the village. They came and introduced themselves to us: Andrew Wilson was the leader of the team and he brought with him two university students, Alex McKie and Nick Andrews, an ex-policeman and writer — Dick Lee — and Colin Wilson who was to be adviser to the group. They also had at their disposal various other volunteer helpers. Andrew's idea had been in the first place to get hold of people in various parts of the country who had particular psychic abilities and encourage them to give up a month of their lives to come and try to solve once and for all the Genette mystery. Altogether between twelve and fourteen people were expected to move into the Village Hall, which they proposed to use as their headquarters.

They called on us to find out what we wanted done and to see whether there was anything that we felt could be done differently. Our discussions continued throughout the morning and as they left they made arrangements to return during the evening.

We still had a holiday booking that had been made before Genette went missing. It was a holiday that she had been looking forward to and we felt that once again we should try to get a message through to whoever was holding her. So the rest of the day was spent circulating a further press release. Its contents were:

To whoever is still holding Genette On 29 November we are going on holiday to Majorca. This was an event which Genette was looking forward to immensely. Please return her to us so that she too can enjoy this trip. Surely you must have put both her and us through enough by now. We are prepared to meet you anywhere, under any conditions to bring about this reunion. Please stop and think what you are doing to our family. If you need help we will make sure that you get it. Please just return our Genette.

To the public It is ironical that one of you somewhere holds the key to this mystery and has not yet come forward with the vital information so badly needed. We ask you to think again. Have you seen either

Genette, the dark-haired man or the maroon car? Has anyone you have contact with been acting unusually since the beginning of August? Do you think somebody else has already told the police the information you know? Have you noticed anything unusual going on in nearby houses over the last three months? If you think you can help, contact the police or telephone Mr Tate.

When we issued this we never expected quite the reaction that we got. That Wednesday morning was absolute hell. It started at 9 o'clock in the morning with a television interview, followed by a reporter from a newspaper, followed by a photographer from another newspaper, followed by another reporter, followed by a radio interview. It became impossible to obtain peace and quiet in the house, so we went into Exeter for a meal.

The rest of the day was all planned out. We had to take the dog and cat to the kennels, make a last visit to the police station to tell them of our whereabouts and then we intended to drive up overnight to be at Luton Airport early in the morning in readiness for our flight to Palma, Majorca.

It was a strange feeling going on holiday without Genette. We had always gone before as a family and this was to have been our first holiday abroad together. We had saved up for a long time for this holiday. We wanted to give the children an opportunity to see one or two other countries before they left school.

When Genette went missing we had intended to cancel the holiday but everyone advised us to take it as we would need it. And so on Thursday morning when Genette had not arrived at Luton Airport (we'd made

The last photographs to be taken of Genette, during a bank holiday outing at the end of May. She was wearing the same trousers when she disappeared

Genette at the end of May

Det Chief Supt Eric Rundle, with Margaret Heavey and Tracey Pratt, the two girls who discovered Genette's abandoned bicycle, reconstructs the scene at the site of Genette's disappearance

The newspaper which Genette was delivering

The Western Times
& Gazette

£1,000 REWARD

for information leading directly to the safe return of

GENETTE TATE

Contact the nearest policeman or ring Woodbury 35111 or 35112 or Exeter 73051

Printed in England by Delderfield Press Ltd., Exmouth, Devon

One of the thousands of posters

An artist's reconstruction of Genette at the time of her disappearance, with her hair cut short

Genette's parents: her mother Sheila, step-mother Violet and John

Genette's pets, Mouser and Tammy

The police operations centre at the Village Hall

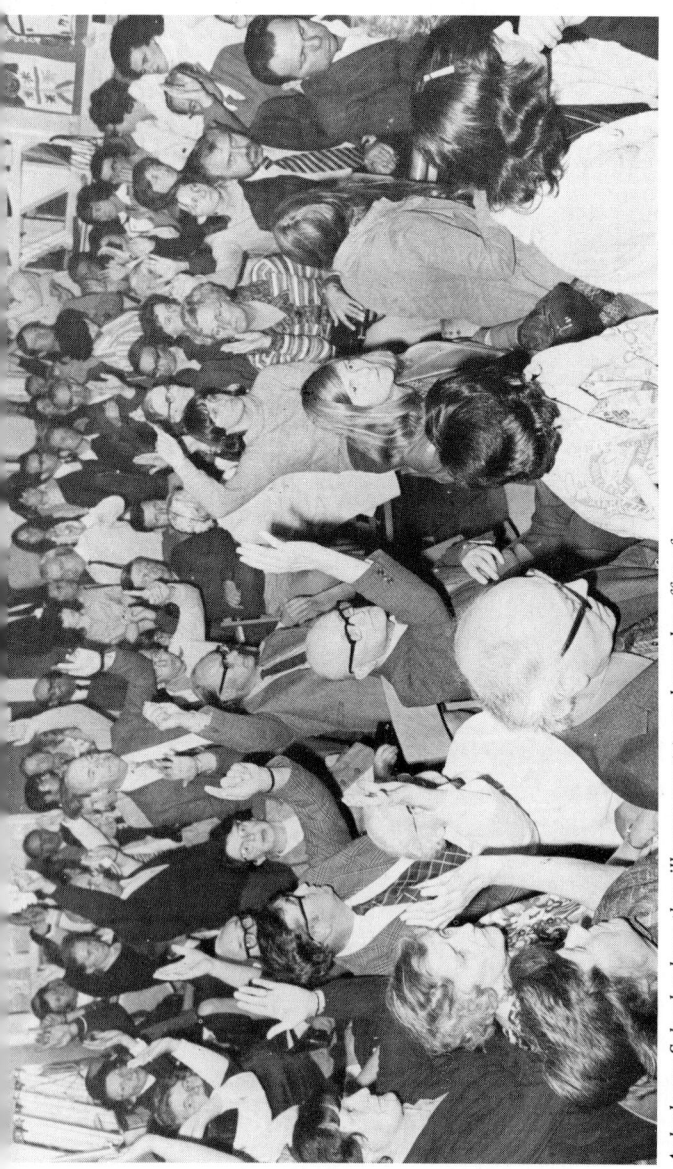

Aylesbeare School, where the villagers meet to endorse the offer of a reward

The Rev Denis Large waits by the telephone with Genette's parents, during his twenty-four-hour appeal for help

The Chief Constable of Devon and Cornwall, Mr John Alderson, joins the search of Woodbury Common

John Tate waits for news of Genette during his twenty-four-hour telephone vigil

Police frogmen search the River Clyst, following information supplied by the Dutch medium, Croiset

Violet and John Tate photographed during a search in late November

Andrew Wilson taking phone calls during his appeal for psychics to come forward

arrangements with the police to get her there should she be found) we waved goodbye to English soil for a week.

5   The Psychic Researchers

We returned home again on the evening of Thursday 7 December. It was a wet and horribly cold night. As we walked across the tarmac I dreaded the moment when we would walk out of Customs Control; there a policeman might be waiting to tell us the news we just did not want to know.

If they had found Genette while we had been away and she was all right, we knew that we would have been contacted and the police would probably have done their best to get her to us. We also thought that if they had found her dead they would probably have kept it from us until we got home. So the relief at finding no one to meet us as we came through the Customs was enormous. We found a telephone and rang Sheila. There had been no news. Sheila only said that there was a lot to tell us when we got home about the psychic research team which had been very busy while we had been away.

Before driving home, we went to Sheila's house in Bristol. She told us that the psychic research team had been appealing for people to come forward to help in a search they were organising for that Sunday. They had also set up a telephone 'hot line' to a special telephone installed at Aylesbeare Village Hall (previously the Police Incident Centre) and let it be known that they wanted to hear from anyone who had had any sort of psychic experience about Genette. Whatever the information, whether a wild dream, anything — they wanted people to phone in.

In a television broadcast Andrew Wilson had asked anyone who might have dreamed of trees, telegraph poles or ponds to let him know so that their information could be collated with that received from other people. It might then be possible to pinpoint the place where Genette had been abducted, or perhaps buried.

The search they were organising had been instigated on the advice of two expert clairvoyants, Nella Jones from Bexleyheath, Kent, and Mr Croiset the Dutchman. Both of them had independently described an area they wished to be searched. Andrew Wilson and his team were asking for volunteers to help in this search. The volunteers were requested to bring their own tools for cutting down undergrowth and told that they had to be warmly dressed, wear wellington boots, leather or plastic gloves and to bring a packed lunch.

On Friday 8 December, Andrew Wilson arrived during the morning to ask us to hold ourselves in readiness to be hypnotised. He said he would send Colin Wilson to collect us when everything was ready. The hypnosis idea came to us totally out of the blue. We were told that they would also be hypnotising the two young girls who had last seen Genette, in the hope that subconsciously they might have seen or heard something useful. In view of this we were only too willing to co-operate.

At about half past two that afternoon Colin Wilson arrived to pick us up and take us to a local inn where the hypnosis sessions were taking place. They decided they would hypnotise Tania first and get from her a full account of all that had happened from the moment she got up in the morning until the moment she had got on the coach to go to Cornwall in the early afternoon. To counteract the possibility of us putting her off or causing her to hold back something, it was decided that we should wait in another room.

After waiting some time, Colin Wilson came to have a chat with us and then went back upstairs. He was obviously very intrigued with whatever had happened so far.

Then our turn came. We were taken upstairs and I was put in a chair. They told us that they had got some very useful information from Tania — something that would probably be quite worthwhile in the long run. We had a cup of tea to make us feel more at ease and then a straightforward and simple test was done on both myself and Violet to see whether in fact we could be hypnotised. The test proved positive on me but negative on Violet.

Then everyone was asked to leave the room, apart from members of the team who were busy operating tape recorders or taking notes, and then the hypnotist began hypnotising me. We talked in general about the health problems I had and he said he felt he might be able to help me with them. I had learnt many years previously how to control pain but had never looked upon it as being a form of self-hypnosis, of the kind that was now being explained to me. And so I went into a trance. It was not like going to sleep: more like a beautiful state of calmness. I was totally aware of everyone around me, of all the noises going on, of the fact that my eyes were closed, and totally aware of what I was doing and saying. I did not feel there was any possibility that I would say anything stupid or do anything out of control. I co-operated with the hypnotist — if you don't co-operate you cannot be hypnotised, as I was soon to find out.

First of all he talked about how I could use parts of my mind that had been lying dormant to heal myself and then he attempted to stimulate my memory by going slowly back in time. He tried to get me to remember something that had happened that day. I couldn't think of a thing. Silly, really, but when asked to remember something on the spur of the moment I found that I couldn't. He persevered, however, and started talking about going up in a lift, one floor at a time. The hypnotist of course did not know that I have a fear of heights and I felt worried about where he was taking me and therefore was not too certain whether I should co-operate or not. He noticed that I was frowning and that my eyes were screwed up tight and that my face was registering concern so he said he would have to check to see how deeply I was under — only to find that I had come out of hypnosis. He came to the conclusion that there were some things in my memory that I did not want to remember. He asked me if I had had any past illness that I had put out of my mind. Naturally in my lifetime there have been many days that I have not wanted to remember. I have no wish to recall the periods I spent in hospital and apparently when one does put up mental blocks of this sort it is impossible, in one session, to go beyond that barrier. Continuous hypnosis sessions make it possible to get over these memory blocks, but apparently we did not have the time. I was therefore disappointed that I could not be hypnotised any further.

We had recently been trying to account for every one of Genette's movements before she went missing. We had satisfied ourselves that we had a fairly clear picture of everything she had done but there was one small thing that was still causing us some concern. During the morning before she disappeared both Tania and Genette had gone to the local post office to buy some sweets and we had been unable to find out what it was that Genette had bought. It was only a little thing but nevertheless a loose end, so it was decided that this information might be got from Tania under hypnosis. She was quickly put out again and taken back to the moment in the post office. After a few questions it was apparent that, although she was watching Genette going through the act of buying, she could not see what she had actually bought. In other words, she could see her handing over the money but did not at the time see her taking whatever the article was; it was very small, something in the middle of her hand. So, it seemed we would never find out what Ginny had actually bought that morning.

The hypnosis session was, I think, the one thing that had a real effect on me. I was amazed at its achievements and believe that considerable benefits could be gained from its further use. It interested me so much that I decided to find out more about it and I have since read a great deal on the subject. I was amazed to discover that hypnosis had been used for carrying out quite difficult and complicated surgery instead of an anaesthetic. It also surprised me to find out how reluctant many people are to having it used for extracting facts from their memories.

To give an example of how accurate it can be: on the particular Saturday morning that Genette went missing Tania sat with her boyfriend and me in the car waiting for Violet and listening to the car radio. Under hypnosis she was able to recall the exact contents of this radio programme many weeks afterwards. This was just one of the many things she had been able to recall.

On the following day, Saturday, we went to Exeter to buy ourselves some new waterproof boots and some thick socks in readiness for the search on the Sunday. This was the first time in my life that I had ever worn out a pair of wellington boots. I had walked so far in the pair I was now discarding that I had worn a hole right through the bottom of them.

It rained most of Saturday afternoon and all Saturday night. When we awoke on Sunday morning it was still damp, wet and miserable. The rain had stopped but the conditions were very wet underfoot, although this did not stop the volunteers from coming. Early in the morning their cars started arriving. The police were back again busily directing traffic to parking sites so that the roads could be kept as clear as possible. We walked up to the Village Hall to find out where to go.

The actual spot that was to be searched had been kept secret, although the area had been described as being roughly one square mile in size. The briefing started and we were told that the area to be searched was very thickly wooded and that the undergrowth had to be cleared right down to the bare ground. We had to put everything we cut down into piles and then the piles would be moved away. Only by doing this could they be absolutely certain that every piece of the wood had been checked meticulously. We then drove to the area set aside for the search party vehicles and parked near a mobile tea van which had arrived to provide refreshments. We walked across the road with our hooks and sticks ready to start work.

It was a rotten, mucky job — thick brambles, lots of fallen trees and a very thick carpeting of rotting wet leaves. We started working close up against the road and gradually began hacking our way into the wood.

We had been divided into groups of twelve, each with a team leader. We busily hacked away at the thick undergrowth. Some of us dragged away bundles of thorns, brambles, twigs and leaves and put them into small piles, which were eventually taken away to make a much bigger mound. Section by section we cleared the ground beneath the trees. We worked for about an hour and a half at a time and then we were told to get a cup of tea and have a break. We found we worked very well under this system — one and a half hours on and half an hour off — and it wasn't long before the lunch-break arrived. We went home, had a quick snack and then came back to the wood again. The area we were searching was Manor Plantation, within a mile of the centre of the village.

One hour into the afternoon the detailed search was completed and the organisers announced they had found what they were looking for. We weren't told what it was at this time. Then we were all asked to assemble on the other side of the track that ran from the roadway through the centre of the wood as we were to carry out a search *en masse* of this area of the wood. We all went back to the road and lined up along the perimeter hedge on the other side of the wood. Stretched out like this we made a very long line of wet, bedraggled people, all with a common aim and each about an arm's length away from his neighbour.

Section leaders were just a bit ahead of us and were given the job of keeping the line straight as it advanced slowly, one pace at a time, through the wood. On the command to advance we set off methodically prodding, pushing, lifting up anything in the way, looking underneath fallen trees, prodding pools of water, investigating everywhere. Every now and again the shout would go up to 'hold the line!'. We would stop where we were until whoever had shouted told us that the query had been investigated.

There was a considerable stir at one stage when we came across a complete skeleton in a freshly dug piece of ground. On investigation, it turned out to be the remains of a deer, but for a while there was chaos as people gathered around to look at this pile of bones. Press photographers seemed to materialise like vultures, their flash-bulbs illuminating the dark wood.

Eventually the line was re-formed and the search continued until we reached the far end of the wood, where we were asked to cross the central path and go to the other side of the wood. Again we walked in a long line through the area that had been cleared during the morning. By this time dusk was falling quite swiftly and we were being hurried along. About halfway through we had to give up — beaten by darkness. We got back on to the main pathway and followed it out of the wood to the main road.

The marines had been helping us, as they had on previous occasions. They had been given the difficult task of moving piles of pit-props from one site to another and checking that there was nothing underneath them. They then sifted through enormous piles of sawdust, where the saw-benches had been running, to make sure there was nothing there.

At the end of the day we were able to give that section of the woods the all-clear. The psychic team then announced that they had been looking for a length of cloth, which had been found, and this was now to be sent for forensic examination. We went home to have a bath and to warm up. This had been a difficult and painstaking search in very cold weather.

I got out the ordnance survey map to have a look at the area we had been searching and was surprised to find it showed a footpath leading from the other side of the village road, right opposite Within Lane, passing between the fields and eventually right into Manor Plantation.

During that week a medium had suggested to us that lead pipes might be of significance and I had been asking around the village trying to find out whether there was anything that might fit the description nearby. It suddenly occurred to me that North Sea gas pipes could have been laid in the area, so I tried to find out. On the Monday morning, whilst talking to one of the villagers, I discovered that gas pipes had been laid through the village and that they ran right across that particular footpath — the one I had been looking at on the map. The following morning I got up early and set off up the path to have a look. Part of the way along I came to a stream and there once again was the picture we had been given some while previously of evergreen trees, a stream too wide to jump and something man-made of wood. Just a few yards from this was where the North Sea gas pipe went underground. I'd imagined in my mind a very big pipe — even big enough to put someone into, but in fact this one was only ten inches in diameter — quite small and in places it ran above ground. There was also, in one of the adjacent fields, a white horse — something else that many mediums and psychics had referred to in one way or another. I thought that the research team should have a look at this area, so I returned to the Village Hall to discuss what I had seen. By then it was time for me to go to work so we arranged to meet early the following morning (Wednesday).

It was a cold, frosty morning, white and sparkling, as I set off to meet the team at the pre-arranged rendezvous outside the 'Blue Anchor', the local village inn. I arrived a few minutes early, and as I waited I was struck by the clean, sharp and new appearance of the frost-covered landscape. Spiders' webs that normally stay invisible on the hedgerows were hanging like delicate strands of silk from one twig to the next. Even the cows in the yard, waiting for their turn to be milked, looked different with the steam wafting from their nostrils.

We started out along the path. As we walked along I pointed out here and there the various things I had noticed. Eventually they decided they would arrange to do an extensive search of the area on either side of this footpath right up to Manor Plantation. I had made up my mind myself that I would continue along this route and walk right through to the plantation and see what could be found in that direction.

Unfortunately the weather was now beginning to turn against us; the days alternated between hard frosts and heavy rain. We could only go out when the weather was fine, although it did clear enough on one day for the team to get a helicopter into the air to search the area from above. They asked Vi to go up with them so that she could point out the various local landmarks. It was an exhilarating experience for her and it was good to see her so much more lively after many weeks of sadness.

It was now approaching Christmas. We had not been looking forward to Christmas very much at all, although for Tania's sake we felt we had to do something about celebrating it. We just couldn't get into the festive mood. We didn't feel like putting up trimmings, but we did get a Christmas tree and Tania busily dressed it. We bought presents and placed them under the tree in the usual way — we even bought them for Genette just in case she should turn up at the last moment. Every day we looked through the Christmas post for her handwriting, hoping there might be a Christmas card to tell us that she was alive and well.

Several newspapers printed features over the Christmas period. One was about the woman who thought she was receiving messages from Genette via automatic writing. We had seen examples of this writing and had compared it with Genette's. We came to the conclusion that, though there were some vague similiarities, they were not enough to convince us that this was something done by Genette.

On Christmas Eve we went to midnight mass at Clyst St Mary. It was a rather moving occasion. It was the first time a communion service has had much of an effect on me. I can't really explain why it was, but I felt totally different afterwards.

We woke on Christmas morning to a day that was much like any other day of the year, but more depressing without the excited chatter of the children opening their Christmas presents, and bouncing on the bottom of our bed, saying 'Look at this! Look at that!' We got up and went downstairs to open our presents. We put the turkey in the oven and, as it was a fine crisp morning, we decided to walk once more along the footpath towards Manor Plantation. We hadn't gone far when it started to rain. My gosh didn't it rain! It came down in bucketfuls! We returned home with all of us, including the dog, absolutely soaked. Tania ran on ahead so she was home long before us. We then sat down to watch the Christmas Day entertainment on the television.

The following morning Violet was on duty and I decided, after taking her to work, that I would carry on the search we had been forced to abandon the day before. I walked with the dog and eventually came to the other end of the path at the beginning of Manor Plantation. Over to my left lay yet another pile of rubbish. I became very annoyed during our searches at coming across so many piles of rubbish: dumped cars, bits of old furniture, polythene sacks in the hedgerows — all the cast-offs of our affluent and so-called educated society left here, there and everywhere, making hideous scars in the beautiful countryside. I walked on through Manor Plantation that day and then turned and retraced my steps, establishing to my own satisfaction that there was no other exit from Within Lane. It is possible to drive a certain distance along this path until it narrows and can then only be followed on foot, and at this point surely the police dogs would have picked up any scents, had there been some.

After Christmas our attention was drawn by snatches of conversation to some stones that had been seen on the day of the big Woodbury Common search. These were large flat pebbles bearing strange markings drawn with a yellow wax crayon and we felt we should go and have a look at them for ourselves. It had taken some time to find out who had actually seen them, but eventually some people agreed to show us the spot.

On Saturday, 31 December, we set off across the fields to see these much discussed stones. There were six of them altogether, laid down in two rows of three. Each stone bore a different marking. Their positioning was most strange, right in the middle of a big hedge (almost a copse). There was a footpath through the middle of this hedge that was apparently used quite frequently by someone. Yet again talk of black magic reared its ugly head.

Naturally the research team were brought in to have a look at them. They took photographs and obtained expert advice on the markings. They also searched for, and managed to find, a seventh stone. According to information given to them about black magic rituals there had to be seven.

The day after the stones were found it snowed and for the rest of the winter the weather really turned against us, stopping our searches completely.

In early January I went to Portugal on a business trip. One afternoon, whilst walking in the bustling streets of Lisbon, I noticed a little boy lying unconscious on the pavement with a begging box beside him and I thought to myself: for as long as something like this can exist, children throughout the world are going to go missing. That child was a very valuable commodity to whoever owned and emptied that box. Amazingly a policeman walked right through the small crowd of people gathered around, stepped over the child and carried on up the street without taking any notice.

On Sunday 14 January, after I had returned home, we spent most of the day talking to a reporter from the *Observer* magazine, having our photographs taken yet again, going back over all the memories and experiences relating to Genette's disappearance.

The cold weather continued with snow and very hard frosts, making searching impossible and even normal journeys difficult and dangerous.

On Sunday, 4 February, the *Observer* magazine

published its article. In it was published our phone number and as a result we had many telephone calls on that day. One call was from a man asking us to tell whoever was in charge of the investigation to pay particular attention to the local graveyard. We received another call from someone who said that the impossible in this situation almost seemed the most likely; that the UFO sightings in the area at the time Genette went missing should not be ignored. And so the calls continued to come in. We were still getting them in the middle of the week.

On the evening of 8 February (Thursday), while I was out, Vi took a phone call from a man who told her that he had known me ten years previously. He said that the time had come when things had to be said. She tried to find out from him what his name was, but all he would say was: 'If you want to find that out you're going to have to come to Ripley'. She was quite upset by the time I got home and really believed that I had been to Ripley (Derbyshire) ten years previously. I had never been there before in my life, but I was sufficiently curious to find out more about this man.

I immediately phoned Sheila, as I had been with her ten years ago, to find out if it brought back any memories for her but we both agreed that we had not known anyone from Ripley at that period of our lives. Plans were made to go and meet this man. They didn't want me to go on my own so all four of us decided to go up on the Saturday night. He had given the name of a public house in Ripley as the meeting place. Fortunately the weather was quite good when we left home and although we encountered some snow as we passed through Somerset the roads were fairly clear.

We collected Sheila from Bristol en route and arrived

in Ripley at about 6.30 that evening. Strangely, the public house, on the outskirts of the town, was still closed and in the darkness it took on a sinister appearance. We decided to try to find something to eat and then to return later on in the evening. We drove back into Ripley and bought some pasties. When we got back to the public house we went in and sat down and waited to see what would happen. We were all on tenterhooks.

Eventually a man walked in and sat down near us. Sheila whispered: 'I bet that's him. He fits that voice perfectly'. Conversation started between us and we soon established that he was the man we had come to see. He said he couldn't talk to us here but would see us later on, so after finishing our drinks we went outside to the car park and found him waiting for us. He asked us to drive him away from the public house, which we did. We found a quiet cul-de-sac further on and pulled in. He then proceeded to tell us his story.

He said there was an organisation called 'The Specials' who abducted girls for breeding purposes. They had two farms, one near the 'White Horse' in Derbyshire, and another in Nottinghamshire. Their big problem was that they were unable to breed females so to continue their clan they would abduct some and this, he said, is what had happened to Genette. It all had to be kept hush-hush and no one was to be told, but a search should be organised. Once he got out of the car we did not know quite what to make of it all. Was it true or was it a figment of his imagination? We pondered on this the whole way back from Ripley. On the journey there we had really thought we were on to something worthwhile. We had thought that here was somebody who knew just where Genette was. Here was someone who could provide us with some vital piece of information, but all we had in return was this incredible story.

On 15 February our hopes were to be raised yet again. At about 9.30pm we had a long-distance telephone call. The voice sounded very distant. In fact it was coming from Southern Ireland, from a man who was sure that he had seen Genette in a nearby shop. He gave us a very good description of her and we were also pretty convinced that he had seen her. It was too late for the police to do anything so the following morning I went into the police station with the information and they made enquiries through the Irish police. Unfortunately the following day the Irish telephone operators went on strike and it was impossible to get information either to or from Ireland. So it was a long time before we got any confirmation one way or the other about this sighting. We almost came to the point of going to Ireland to find out for ourselves. We had ascertained the price of the return air-fare tickets and were making arrangements for the journey, when the police heard that it was a case of mistaken identity. Our hearts sank.

We were now approaching the six-months' anniversary of the date of Genette's disappearance. It was our intention on this day to hold a Press conference to try to get public attention back on to our situation. So on Sunday 18 February, exactly six months to the day since Genette had gone, members of the press, radio and television arrived at our house. We had a lovely log fire burning in the grate and the dog, Tammy, was asleep on the hearthrug. Now that she was deaf she was oblivious to most things going on around her; when the doorbell rang she did not even move. Not so many months ago there would have been sheer bedlam — but not any more. We put the Sunday roast in to the oven on the automatic timer so that we could have a meal at the end of the Press conference.

The scene in our country cottage was like that in many other country cottages in Devon on a Sunday morning, that is until an observant eye noticed the books scattered around the room: the *Reader's Digest Book of Strange Stories and Amazing Facts*, the *Mystic Dream Book — 2,500 Dreams Explained*, a copy of Colin Wilson's *Mysteries*. There was an eerie significance about these books in our house. Ours was no ordinary domestic scene on that cold and damp Sunday morning — we were about to put ourselves through the ordeal of yet another Press conference.

I started off by talking about the weather and apologising for it, hoping that no one had to travel through snow to get to us. I then gave the reason for calling the Press conference, quite a simple one — it was six months since Genette had disappeared. 'We want to remind the public about Genette. We also want to get over the fact that this could happen to anyone's child. We were the unfortunate victims. It could so easily happen to anyone — from a top executive to a dustman. There's also been a lot of talk about Genette being dead. We want to tell the world that there are no more facts available now than there were at 3.30pm on that Saturday afternoon when she went missing. All we have heard are theories. There is nothing to prove she is dead. There is nothing to say she is alive. We can only stress that we want to hear from people who think they have seen Genette. We know that there are people who think they have, but hesitate to come forward. Rather like the Bible statement: ¿"There are those who have eyes and see not. There are those who have ears and hear not".'

I had prepared for this conference the following

appeal:

> *To anyone either with Genette or holding her against her will* Make contact with us in any way you like, by phone, letter, to the police, the Press or however. Just as long as we know. You have made us suffer long enough.
>
> *To Genette* If you can make contact, even a postcard would do. If you don't want to write to us, contact Aunty Ethel or one of your grandparents, just as long as we know you are safe and well.
>
> *To the public* Keep looking for Genette. If you think you have seen her contact us or the police. Don't give up looking and don't presume she is dead until it is proved.

At this Press conference we announced our intention to form an organisation to help the families of missing children, which would also take a fresh look at the whole missing children problem.

The newspaper reporters filed out, we posed for yet another barrage of flash-bulbs as the cameramen took their turn. Outside, we answered questions from a TV news crew. Finally, they too were gone and peace returned to our home as we sat down to enjoy our Sunday lunch.

6 The Occult Detectives
Colin Wilson

Saturday, 19 August 1978 was a sunny day, the end of a week of superb weather. Consulting my journal, I discover that I dozed on the lawn for an hour, then set out to pick up my children, who had gone to Mevagissey to spend their pocket money. A hundred miles away, in Aylesbeare, Genette Tate was setting out on her bicycle to collect newspapers for the afternoon delivery. And by the time I returned home from Mevagissey, at half past three, Genette had vanished, and the search for her was already beginning. It was the beginning of one of the largest police hunts that has ever taken place in England.

My own involvement was a matter of chance. In the middle of the previous week, the psychic, Robert Cracknell, arrived at our house; he was en route for a caravan site at Land's End with his family. Since the previous year, I had been trying to find a publisher for his autobiography; on the Thursday before Genette's disappearance, we had spent the afternoon talking about an introduction that I intended to write for the book, and I had been fascinated by his account of his involvement in the 'Southern Organs' case, when he had been able to tell the police the precise whereabouts of confidence swindlers who had absconded with a large sum of money belonging to subscribers. But even more fascinating was his story of how a reporter friend had phoned him to ask whether he had any 'impressions' about the murder of an Australian girl named

Janey Shepherd. Bob knew nothing of Janey Shepherd, except what he had read in the newspapers — that she had vanished in the Queensway area of London, and that her mini had later been found abandoned. Yet Bob's 'impressions' about the murder — she was found a month later in a wood near St Albans — were so accurate that a police inspector hurried round to his house, suspecting that he could be the killer. Cracknell was soon able to convince them that his knowledge came from 'psychic' sources — and that, in any case, the murderer was already in police custody. A man had been arrested a few days before — for rape — and the police already suspected that he might be the murderer of Janey Shepherd. (He is now serving a seven-year sentence; the Janey Shepherd murder is still officially unsolved.)

When Bob Cracknell returned to his caravan site that afternoon, we lost touch — the site was not on the telephone. And when, the following Monday, I saw television film of the search for Genette Tate, I found myself wishing that I could contact him. This was not simply a desire to help find the missing teenager; it was obvious that, if Cracknell could help to find Genette, he would have no difficulty finding a publisher for his autobiography.

So when he phoned me, the following Wednesday, I asked him whether he had any psychic 'impressions' about the missing girl. 'What missing girl?' He had spent the previous few days lying on beaches; their hired car had no radio, and there were no newspapers at the camping site. This was the first he had heard of Genette's disappearance.

I told him the basic details, and he said he'd like to 'have a go'. The first necessity was to place this on record. I asked him to phone me back in an hour's time. Then I rang a friend — Peggy Archer — at the BBC in Plymouth, and told her the story. She thought it would make an interesting item for the 'Morning Sou'West' programme the next morning. When Bob rang back, I gave him the BBC's number, and asked him to ring Peggy.

An hour later, he rang me again. The BBC had interviewed him over the telephone, and the interview had been, apparently, a great success. Bob's impression was that Genette was dead — that she had been abducted by someone in a car — and that her body would be found before the following Sunday, within twenty miles of her home. His impression was that the man was driving a blue car, and that he had a record of mental illness. In fact, the newspaper that morning had mentioned that the police were trying to trace a blue car. But Bob had not seen any newspapers for a week, and I had not mentioned it.

The interview went out the next morning — I was still asleep and missed it. But later that morning, Peggy Archer rang me again. The tape of the interview had been sent to the police, and they were so interested in some of his comments that they wanted him to come to Aylesbeare, and see if he could pick up any more 'impressions' at the site of the disappearance. Could I contact him? Unfortunately this was impossible. All I could do was to send a telegram to the camp site, and hope he would ring me before mid-afternoon, when the last train for Plymouth left from Penzance. In fact, the train had left by the time he rang. I could only ask him to contact the BBC, and decide whether he wanted to spend a day of his holiday searching for a missing girl. There were some obvious difficulties. He had to return to London within forty-eight hours. It was asking a great deal to expect him to travel to Aylesbeare, then back to Land's End, on the last day of his holiday.

The BBC was persuasive. He decided to cut short his holiday by a day, and drive out to Aylesbeare. On his way there, he would come and call for me — for the police invitation apparently included myself.

Which is how, at midday the following day — Friday, 25 August — we came to find ourselves at the police incident room in Aylesbeare, accompanied by BBC reporter Bob Forbes, and by Chief Inspector Don Crabb, second-in-command of the investigation.

Aylesbeare is not the kind of village you would remember if you drove through it in a car. With its ugly pre-fab houses, it looks like a bit of a Birmingham suburb that has been dumped in the midst of Devonshire fields. The village straggles along one main street, with the village hall at one end, and a pub — the Blue Anchor — at the other. The pub stands on the corner of Within Lane, where Genette disappeared. The Village Hall had been utilised as the incident room; when we arrived the lawn was crowded with dozens of policemen and policewomen, eating their lunch.

Chief Inspector Don Crabb took us inside the incident room, and showed us Genette's bicycle; it looked new, and the closest examination revealed no scratches or dents. The table in the middle of the room was covered by a huge ordnance survey map of the area. As he stood by the table, Bob asked suddenly if there was a place called Broad Oak in the area. Don Crabb had no idea; but one of the helpers in the room said there *was* such a place, and pointed it out to us on the map. Bob said the name had simply come into his head. He also admitted that he *might* have unconsciously registered it as he looked at the map. He said that the name 'John' had also come into his head in connection with the case. In fact, there were two Johns: Genette's father, and the boy whose newspaper round Genette had taken over when she disappeared. Neither were suspects.

Don Crabb drove us to Within Lane, to show us the spot where Genette had vanished. And I began to understand the complexities of the case. Within Lane is a typical Devon country lane, wide enough — along most of its length — for only one car. About a hundred yards along from the village end, the lane widens for a dozen yards or so, and there is space at the side for two or three cars. This is the spot where Genette's bicycle was found, lying on its side, the newspapers scattered over the ground behind it.

Before Don Crabb could start to give us the details, Cracknell held up his hand. 'I'd rather not know anything at this stage — it's easy to mix up impressions.' He wandered off, his head lowered, walking slowly and looking from side to side — he reminded me of a dog trying to pick up a scent. Don Crabb and I stood by the car, and he told me the story of that Saturday afternoon six days ago. Genette had cycled along Within Lane shortly before three, to pick up the newspapers at the White Horse, on the Sidmouth road. On her way back, at a bridge over a tiny stream, she had paused to speak with two friends from the village — Margaret Heavey and Tracey Pratt; two visitors to the area — a woman and her daughter — had also spoken to the girls, enquiring about local discotheques. Tracey persuaded Genette to hand over the newspaper that would be delivered at her home; Genette objected that she had to collect the money, but Tracey pointed out that she would be home by the time Genette arrived at the house. So Genette cycled off down Within Lane, towards Aylesbeare, while Margaret and Tracey strolled on, reading the newspaper and discussing a story about a UFO that was prominent on the front page. About five minutes later, they rounded a bend in the lane, and saw Genette's bicycle lying on its side, about twenty yards away. Their first thought was that Genette had climbed over the hedge to 'spend a penny'; they reached the bicycle and called her name. One of the girls said the back wheel was still turning, as if it had only just been laid on its side. The newspapers were on the ground — having fallen out of the saddle bag — but were not widely scattered. It was as if the bicycle had been laid on its side fairly quickly, but not violently. The girls called, then began to wonder if Genette was playing a joke and hiding. Then, when they could find no sign of her, they began to feel nervous; one asked the other 'Are you thinking what I'm thinking?' — that Genette could have been kidnapped, or even spirited away by a flying saucer. At this point, they decided to run to the village for help.

It was a puzzling set-up, as I could see at once. Let us suppose that a man had been sitting in a parked car at the side of Within Lane, and that he called to Genette as she went past, grabbed her, and pushed her inside the car or into the boot. He must then have driven off towards the village, because if he had driven the other way, the car would have been noticed by Margaret and Tracey, and probably by the two holidaymakers. At the Blue Anchor end of Within Lane, he had a choice of turning left or right — it is a T-junction. He would hardly be likely to turn left, and drive through the village, in case someone noticed him. But, Don Crabb told me, there had been a number of people who had been in a position to observe him if he turned right at the T-junction. And none of them had noticed a car at about that time. Moreover, it seemed to me that to attack a young girl at that particular spot would be a risky venture. It is overlooked by the upper storey of houses across the field — although it is doubtful whether anyone would be looking out of a bedroom window at 3.20 on a hot Saturday afternoon — and people might walk — or even drive — around the bend in the lane at any moment.

Bob Cracknell returned as we stood talking. His own impression, he said, was that Genette had been knocked off her bicycle by a man, about five yards away from the spot where the bicycle had been found. The man had hit her on the right temple. He had probably called out her name — he may have been someone who knew her. (Don Crabb pointed out that this was not necessary — Genette had her name embroidered on her shirt, and he could have seen it as she cycled by on her way to collect the newspapers.) Cracknell's impression was that the man had then carried her over the opposite hedge into a field. Sexual assault, he said, was probably the motive, but he felt that Genette had not been raped. Perhaps the man was frightened when he realised he had killed her or knocked her unconscious.

Cracknell's impression was that the man was a labouring type, perhaps a farm labourer, and that he was of slightly subnormal intelligence. Later, when the girls had run off to raise the alarm, he had carried Genette out of the field, across Within Lane, and into the opposite field (behind the 'car park'), where he had then carried her away from the village, parallel with the lane. His impression was that Genette was concealed now in a pond somewhere nearby.

Don Crabb listened to all this seriously, and discussed the various possibilities. It struck me as interesting that he was willing to listen to a 'psychic'. In most well-known murder mysteries, the police receive dozens of messages from psychics, and they seldom take them seriously. At the same time, I could understand why Don Crabb should be willing to pursue any line that seemed promising. Search teams had scoured the area for five miles around and investigated every pond — most of them were little more than puddles after the hot summer; they had found absolutely nothing. There were no clues of any kind ...

Cracknell said he would like to talk to Genette's parents, and borrow some items of her clothing. The ability to receive 'impressions' from clothing and personal belongings is called 'psychometry', and a surprisingly large number of people seem to possess it. Some are famous clairvoyants — like Peter Hurkos and Gerard Croiset, who have frequently helped the police to solve murder cases. Yet perfectly ordinary people often prove to have latent psychometric powers, just as (I am convinced), most of us are able to use a dowsing rod to divine for water. (In my own experience, nine out of ten people can dowse.)

We drove round the corner to the cottage occupied by the Tates, a stone's throw from the village hall. John Tate answered the door, a small man, younger than I had expected, with a beard. When I was introduced to him, he surprised me by saying: 'I've got one of your daughter's drawings on my wall'. He pointed to a framed picture. I learned then — what I had not realised before — that the Tates had previously lived in our village in southern Cornwall, before moving to Devon. They had, in fact, actually been to our house —

with Genette — to help supervise a children's party, although my wife and I had been in America at the time. It was an odd coincidence.

I was worried about intruding into the home of a family whose child is missing. It is one thing to see a man on television appealing for information about his missing daughter, another to walk into his house when his head is still full of misery and anxiety. Still, I was relieved to find that John Tate seemed calm and normal. His wife, Genette's stepmother Vi, offered us a cup of tea. Bob asked her if she would show him Genette's bedroom, and Don Crabb and I sat talking to John Tate. He told us about the chair he was sitting in — a vibratory chair for the relief of back pains; I gathered that he had worked as a salesman of such chairs. He struck me as a man of more than average intelligence, and I noted books on psychology and sociology lying around the room. He seemed to be taking Genette's disappearance unusually well; most parents in such a situation would be distraught and frantic. Yet that, I suspected, could have been because he had convinced himself that Genette was still alive, and would come back home. All the same, I felt a brute for sitting in his house, drinking his tea, when he had more than enough problems to think about.

Inevitably, in a situation like this, John Tate had been on the list of suspects; but already, by the time we arrived in Aylesbeare, the police had ruled him out. It was not simply that he had no motive for harming his own daughter; he also had an alibi that was confirmed by many witnesses. On the morning of Genette's disappearance, he had driven his step-daughter Tania, Genette's step-sister, into Exeter — she was going away on holiday to Perranporth — then collected Vi from the hospital where she worked, and taken her shopping. They arrived back after Margaret and Tracey had raised the alarm about Genette's disappearance.

I was relieved when Bob Cracknell came downstairs with Vi Tate; we thanked them for the tea, and left. Genette's room had failed to produce any new 'impressions' about her disappearance; from this point of view, the visit had been a waste of time. He had handled Genette's clothing, and again had the impression that she was dead, and was lying in water. But his psychic impressions were now being overlaid by what we had been told about the case. There seemed no point in staying in Aylesbeare any longer. It had been an interesting, but on the whole unfruitful, visit.

During the next two days — Saturday and Sunday — I listened to every news bulletin, hoping to hear that Genette had been found — either dead or alive. If she was, in fact, found within that time limit, it would certainly be a major triumph for Bob Cracknell — and an excellent point with which to conclude his introduction. But by Monday morning, it was clear that he had been wrong about the finding of a body. This, at least, left open the possibility that she was still alive.

As the months went by, this became less likely. The police search still continued, and there were periodic appeals for information on television. The two women holidaymakers had, apparently, been hypnotised, and had come up with a description of a car that had passed them in Within Lane shortly before Genette rode off; they had even, according to the newspapers, described a suspect. Apart from that, it seemed clear that the police had no promising leads.

Some time in November, my wife told me that a TV

director wanted to speak to me on the telephone about Genette Tate. The man introduced himself as Andrew Wilson, and told me that he wanted to make a programme about Genette's disappearance, using information from various psychics. Would I be interested in taking part? He was surprised when I told him that I had already spent some time in Aylesbeare with Bob Cracknell. He had never heard of Bob, but as far as he was concerned, the more psychics on the case the better.

It sounded an interesting project. My friend Dan Farson, television broadcaster and writer, had agreed to take part. So had Dick Lee, a retired detective, who had become well known for his part in the drugs case, 'Operation Julie', about which he had written a successful book. There was a frogman on the team, and a corps of volunteers from Exeter University. They planned to start in early December.

My own role in the project was not entirely clear — he wanted me on the team because I had written a book on the 'occult', and was also the author of a number of books on criminology — but it sounded promising. From my own point of view it would be an interesting follow-up to my visit with Cracknell.

On Friday, 1 December 1978, I set out to drive to Aylesbeare, en route to Cardiff (where I was to talk to a producer about a play I was writing.) Around 1 o'clock, I found my way to the Blue Anchor, where I met Andrew Wilson — a tall, bearded man, rather younger than I expected — and Dick Lee. Don Crabb was there; so was Det Chief Supt Proven Sharpe, head of Devon and Cornwall CID. Dan Farson sent a telegram saying he was unable to make it. We drank several glasses of wine, then moved down to the Village Hall, where a

Thames Television crew was waiting to film us. The room where I had examined Genette's bicycle was now bare and empty. Our own 'incident room' — we were apparently calling ourselves the Aylesbeare Special Research Unit — was the smaller room next door, which was easier to heat in that icy winter. We sat around a table, and were briefed — in front of the camera — by Don Crabb and Mr Sharpe, who told us the story of Genette's disappearance in detail. The only new information, as far as I was concerned, was that the two girls, Margaret and Tracey, had seen a car in the lane at the time they were talking to Genette. Both of them felt that it was driven by an elderly couple. The two holidaymakers, apparently, vaguely remembered seeing a second car in the lane, not long after the other. The police were anxious to trace this second car, but so far had no leads.

We all trooped around to Within Lane, followed by the TV crew, and Don Crabb again explained the circumstances of Genette's disappearance. A car containing two women was obliged to halt for us; one of the women came and stood beside me and asked me what was going on. When I told her, she mentioned that *she* thought she might have seen the man who had abducted Genette. On the evening before the disappearance, she said, she had been standing in the centre of Exeter. A man in a red car had passed her slowly, and stared at her in a peculiar manner — perhaps wondering if she was 'available'. A few minutes later, he passed her again — he was obviously cruising round the block — and his manner struck her as so suspicious that she looked at the number of his car. Unfortunately, she had no pencil or paper, so she committed it to memory, determined to write it down as soon as she got home; but on the way she stopped to talk to a friend and forgot it. When she heard about Genette's disappearance, she was immediately convinced that this was the man who was responsible.

The story interested me. I remembered that the holidaymakers had seen a red car in Within Lane shortly before Genette vanished; they had later recalled more details under hypnosis. A few weeks earlier, I had taken part in a local television programme with a hypnotist called Joe Keeton, who had 'regressed' a nurse until she was describing her life as a Devon girl named Kitty Jay, who committed suicide in the eighteenth century. Could Joe Keeton perhaps bring back the memory of the car number plate? It seemed worth trying. The woman — whose name was Hazel — said she was willing to be hypnotised, and I took her address and telephone number.

The afternoon was getting dark and cold. With Nella — a clairvoyant — in the lead, we all trooped along Within Lane. Like Bob Cracknell, Nella was moving in a slow, abstracted way, as if listening for something. At one point she stopped, and pointed to the hedge, saying that she had an impression that a car, travelling at a great speed, had bounced against it immediately after Genette's disappearance. Because she had asked us to tell her nothing about the precise details, nobody told her that this was impossible — since the two little girls were walking down the lane at the time, and would have noticed a car in a hurry. Nella also mentioned that she had a clear mental picture of a field with a pond, and a wood fire. A few hundred yards further along the lane we came across just such a field; the remains of a large bonfire were still smouldering in the middle, and there was a pond in the corner. Our searchers splashed intrepidly into the pond and prodded around with long sticks; but they found nothing. I have to admit that my own expectations were low. Although I believe in the existence of paranormal powers, I somehow had no faith in their ability to find Genette. The hypnotist seemed an altogether better bet.

Two days later, on my way back from Cardiff, I again stopped at Aylesbeare. Sim, our volunteer on the telephone, handed me a large pile of messages and letters. Local television had publicised our venture, and appealed for information — 'paranormal' or otherwise. Most of my letters were 'paranormal'. One lady had dreamed that she saw Genette being forced into the boot of a white car with some distinctive marking. Later, driving along the motorway, she saw the identical car in front of her. She had noted down its licence number. I passed it on to the policeman on duty to check. (Later, he told me that the lead came to nothing.) Another letter — from a clairvoyant — said that she had 'seen' Genette being buried in a churchyard, in a grave in which someone else had recently been interred. This struck me as an ingenious way of concealing a body; the policeman made a note to take the tracker dogs around local churchyards, sniffing all newly dug graves for signs of a corpse near the surface. (This was also done, and produced no result.) Other letters described visions — or dreams — in which Genette was buried in remote barns, compost heaps and sewage works. (In fact, we had checked two lots of local sewage works on the previous afternoon.)

The obvious way to deal with this flood of information was to start a kind of index, with entries under each heading: 'cars', 'ponds', 'rivers', 'compost heaps', 'murder', 'accident', and so on. One of the girls did this. One interesting letter pointed out that a certain local man had a police record, and several convictions for drunken driving. He was also, it said, a frogman. Some article belonging to him had been found in a search of Woodbury Common. The writer suggested that he might have knocked down Genette accidentally and — because such an accident would endanger his licence, and his job involved driving — had decided to dispose of the body. The objection to this theory was that Genette's bicycle was undamaged, and the girls in Within Lane would probably have heard a crash. But we passed on the letter to Don Crabb, who eventually eliminated the suspect.

Dick Lee and I interviewed the two little girls, Margaret and Tracey, and I had a chance to see Dick's method of work. He is a pleasant, relaxed sort of man, with a kindly smile, and he asks questions in such a frank and friendly manner that witnesses seem to experience an immediate desire to be as helpful as possible. Puffing thoughtfully at his pipe, there is more than a touch of BBC television's Maigret about him. But as we took Tracey and Margaret — separately — over their route of that August afternoon, I observed how carefully he was noting their answers, and how apparently casual — and undirected — questions would be repeated in a different form a few minutes later, to try to sniff out inconsistencies and contradictions.

The girls were able to tell us nothing that they had not already told the police. What emerged was a picture of a rather aimless, boring Saturday afternoon, with nothing in particular to do; a stroll along Within Lane, discussing Tracey's boyfriend (whom she hoped to see on the farm where he was working), and a conversation on the bridge, where they threw stones into the stream and talked about what they would like to do when they left school. Dick asked them to sit down exactly where they had sat that afternoon, their feet dangling over the stream, and a moment later, I understood his motive when he asked them whether they would notice a car passing behind them if they were facing away from it, and engaged in conversation. The girls admitted that they might not.

We asked the children if they would be willing to submit to hypnosis; both of them agreed; so did their parents. At this point, we were rejoined by Andrew, who had been on Aylesbeare Common with a marine search team. Dick, Andrew and I adjourned to the pub where they were staying — the Halfway Inn — to warm ourselves up with a drink.

Andrew was distinctly gloomy. To begin with, he had dismissed the television team. It seemed that ITV had agreed to finance the Research Unit with a sum of several thousand pounds, in the hope of getting a programme out of it. (Ideally, of course, a programme that would conclude with the finding of the missing girl.) But they were already making excuses to delay paying the money; the reason, Andrew said, was that they wanted to impose some of their own conditions. To begin with, they wanted to suggest that the failure to find Genette had been due to police inefficiency. Andrew flatly disagreed. Not only had the police done everything possible to find her; they had also kept up the search just about four times as long as any other police force in Europe would have done. (A French police expert who came to Aylesbeare told Don Crabb that they would have given up after three weeks, assuming her to be dead or out of the area.) Finally, Andrew had lost his temper and told them to go to hell.

So now we had no backers and no money. This made no difference whatever to me, or to Dick Lee — neither of us expected to be paid. But it was bound to limit the activity of the rest of the team.

There was another problem. Chief Superintendent Eric Rundle — Don Crabb's superior — was thoroughly hostile to our whole venture; he had told Andrew that he thought we were 'a lot of cowboys' (whatever that meant), and intimated that he felt we were in it for money or publicity. Andrew assured him that no one on the team intended to make money out of the case; but apparently he was unconvinced. Without police co-operation we were obviously going to have a difficult time ...

I asked Andrew the question that had been in my mind since the previous day — when I learned that he was *not* the director of the television programme: why *was* he doing all this? I had originally assumed that it was simply a matter of an interesting piece of television; but now, it seemed, he had dismissed the film crew. So what were we all doing in Aylesbeare?

The answer, it seemed, was that this was a kind of personal crusade. Andrew speaks fluent Dutch, and works as a television director in Holland. He had approached the Dutch clairvoyant Gerard Croiset, to see if he had any 'impressions' of how Genette disappeared. I had worked with Croiset myself — on the case of a disappearance that took place in Scotland — and knew something about his method of working. Croiset had handled some article of Genette's clothing, then taken a pencil, and drawn a line on an ordnance survey map of the Aylesbeare area. Andrew was excited to discover that, although he had told Croiset nothing about the terrain, Croiset had made a cross within a few yards of the spot where Genette's bicycle was found. The line continued into the field next to the 'car park' — the field that Bob Cracknell claimed the murderer had been in — and around in a wide circle, until it ended at a spot about half a mile from Aylesbeare. Croiset said Genette was dead, and that her body was lying under water, close to some kind of grid.

Andrew had also been in touch with the London clairvoyant, Nella Jones, who had no knowledge of the terrain either. But Nella had drawn a sketch map as well, giving her impressions of the route taken by the killer — she too believed Genette had been murdered. And the similarities between her map and Croiset's were striking. It was at that point that Andrew had decided to set up his own research unit.

But it seemed that the past twenty-four hours had been doubly disappointing. Not only had he lost his financial backing; the routes drawn by Croiset and Nella had also proved to be totally impracticable. Croiset's route went through impassable Devon hedgerows, and ended in the middle of a field, with no sign of water. Nella's route (if I remember correctly) ended in a farmyard; but the compost heap there revealed no sign of a body. Croiset had agreed to come over to England if his map failed to provide any clues; but it would be impossible before mid-January. Meanwhile, we had a large team of helpers, an increasing pile of letters from clairvoyants and visionaries, and no real clue to what had happened on that August afternoon ...

As I drove home that night, leaving Andrew and Dick — and the frogman Steve — to their Spartan quarters, I turned over the problem in my mind. Now I was beginning to get the threads of the investigation into my hands, I could understand its complexity. And I had a feeling that ordinary logic would probably produce better results than checking through hundreds of letters. The terrain itself should provide the basic clues. To begin with, we had to assume that Genette was taken away by car — even Bob Cracknell was now coming around to this opinion. But if the man was in an unlikely spot like Within Lane, then it seemed likely that he knew the area. It *was* possible, of course, that a sex maniac with a record of mental illness was driving aimlessly around the Devon area on that August afternoon, and had happened to see a solitary little girl on her bicycle. But why would he stop his car in Within Lane, within a hundred yards of a village? Why not some remote spot on the Common, or near a beach?

Now if he knew the area, then he must have had some plan in mind. He would be unlikely to drive through the village, for fear of being seen; this meant he probably turned right, towards Aylesbeare Common. In fact, a man who knew the area would almost certainly head for Aylesbeare or Woodbury Common — the two are adjacent. Even on an August afternoon, there would be plenty of lonely spots there, and he might drive his car direct to one of these. Admittedly, the two Commons had been extensively searched. But both are enormous. And then, the man may have concealed the body for a week or so, then removed it elsewhere. Two of the letters I had received suggested that Genette's body had been moved within two weeks of her death.

In that case, we were searching for a local man. But the police had, presumably, checked on everybody in the area with a record of sex crime or violence. Our best hope, it seemed, lay in uncovering some new facts through hypnosis. If Hazel could be induced to remember that car number ...

At home, the following day, I wrote to Joe Keeton, outlining the problem and asking if he would be willing to come down and hypnotise Hazel and the two children. Twenty-four hours later, Joe rang me from Liverpool, saying he'd be happy to help. If Hazel had really memorised the number plate, then it could be recovered under hypnosis, because the memory carries a photographic record of everything we have seen and heard, even unconsciously.

That sounded promising. Joe would come over the following week; he was busy until then. So, for that matter, was I. Andrew was clearly hoping that I would go to stay at the Halfway House and take a more active part in the search; but he obviously had no idea of the problems of an overworked writer. On the day I arrived back from Aylesbeare, the *New York Times* had phoned me to ask if I could produce a 2,500-word article on Bernard Shaw and Feminism before the weekend. I was supposed to be writing a three-act play for the Ty Coch Theatre Company in Cardiff, to be presented at the end of January, and I had so far written only the first act — the play was going into rehearsal in three week's time. I was being nagged by my publisher to revise a book on Wilhelm Reich, and by the BBC to finish a long novel which was to be serialised as a television play. Andrew was obviously disappointed that I wasn't there, on the spot; but then, Andrew worked only half the year as a TV producer, and spent the other half 'resting'. Anyway, the whole project struck me as oddly pointless and aimless. Of course, *if* we succeeded in finding Genette, everybody would congratulate him on a brilliant hunch. But, as far as I could see, our chances

...aper — *her* own sentence, which would [ena]ble her to go back to the beach whenever she [sh]e would have to repeat the words in exactly [...] (otherwise, said Joe, it would be too easy, [she m]ight accidentally hypnotise herself in some [...] situation) — and he wrote them down on a [pa]per. 'I am now going to my beach for X [... sh]e was to insert the number herself), and [wak]e up I shall feel relaxed and completely [...]

[At this po]int Joe roused her from the trance. Then he [...] the sheet of paper on which he had written [...] She read it, closed her eyes, and [...] went to sleep again. A few minutes later [...], with a bright, charming smile; in answer [to a ques]tion, she said she felt marvellous. She had [...] her beach.

[It was] time to get down to the serious business. [...] Joe placed her in a trance. Then he told [her the] afternoon of Saturday the 19th of August, [...] year. The time is now three o'clock. [Where are]you?' 'In Within Lane.' 'And who is [with you? T]racey ...' Step by step, Joe took her along [th]e bridge, making her repeat the conversa[tion. If] I wanted to ask a question, we only had [to catch]eye and interpose; Margaret answered us [through] Joe. We asked her about the sounds she [heard;] she mentioned a tractor in a field over to [...] described Genette riding up to them as [they came b]ack up the hill from the bridge, and the [...] bout the newspaper as Genette walked [past;] he described the car that went past them [and had] to stand in to the side of the lane. Joe [said a man] was driving; she said she couldn't see —

were minimal; the police had already done the real work.

Still, I kept my doubts to myself. And a week later, with the article and another half-act of the play completed, I drove back to Aylesbeare, to watch Joe Keeton in action.

In fact, Joe had arrived there on the previous day; I had been in hospital for my annual check-up, so could not attend. But it seemed that I hadn't missed much. He had been along to Hazel's home to try and hypnotise her, but it had been impossible. She had been too tense and nervous; after an hour, Joe had been forced to give up.

When I arrived — at a pub in Newton Poppleford where the session was due to take place — Margaret was already there. She was an intelligent little girl, younger than Tracey. There were also half a dozen other people present in the sitting-room over the public bar. These included Andrew Wilson and Dick Lee, a policeman and a doctor — the latter was present to provide medical supervision — and two secretaries. Joe Keeton, a large reassuring man with a north-country accent, was already talking when I arrived. He was explaining to Margaret about hypnosis — that it was not some kind of magic, or an infallible lie detector, but merely an attempt to get through to her unconscious mind, to find out things it had forgotten. It was like watching a stage entertainment; we all sat there, completely absorbed.

First of all, said Joe, he was going to try a simple experiment to see if Margaret was a good hypnotic subject. He asked her to close her eyes, then stretch out both her hands in front of her, one palm upwards, the other with the thumb pointing to the ceiling. He wanted she wasn't looking. Joe told her to look now, and she said she saw a middle-aged couple. He asked her to look down at the licence plate and read it. She read out a number, slowly and deliberately. We glanced at one another, hoping that this might be the breakthrough we all hoped for. Dick interrupted to ask whether she and Tracey left the lane at any point, even for a moment. Did they, perhaps, climb over a gate to 'spend a penny'? Margaret firmly denied this. And she also denied seeing a second car. She went on to describe finding the bicycle, calling Genette's name, looking over the hedge into the field, then into the opposite field. (For some reason, neither of them thought to look up the track a few yards back along the lane — by the field Bob Cracknell said the man had dragged Genette into.)

Finally, Joe woke her up. On the whole, it had been disappointing. Margaret had answered every question fully. But except for the car number, she had not told us anything that she had not already told Dick and me as we walked with her along Within Lane.

It was now getting close to lunch time. Margaret and her mother left. Tracey was due after lunch. While we waited, the girls asked Joe if he could give them a 'beach' too. Both proved to be excellent hypnotic subjects; within a few minutes, both were breathing deeply, wearing beautific smiles as they wiggled their toes in the sand and turned their faces up to the sun.

Later, it was Tracey's turn. She struck me as tense and nervous. Although only fourteen, she seemed much more grown-up than Margaret, a young lady with her own ideas, and a will of her own. She was harder to hypnotise than Margaret, but after ten minutes she seemed relaxed enough. I found myself wondering whether she was genuinely asleep, or whether she was pretending, simply to oblige us. There was no way of telling. Hypnotised people do not speak in a slow, dreamy voice; they sound very much as they do when awake. Again, Joe took her over the same ground as Margaret; the walk along Within Lane to the bridge, the conversation with Genette and the two holiday-makers. When the car passed, she was also asked to look through the windscreen. She said the driver was a man, and that he was alone. She also read the number plate, figure by figure; we all noticed that she gave a different number from the one Margaret had read aloud. The police sergeant noted down everything she said. The rest of us were beginning to feel that all this effort was leading nowhere. Like Margaret, Tracey told us nothing that we did not already know.

I offered to drive Tracey and her mother back to Aylesbeare. And at this point, Andrew asked me to call on John Tate, and bring him back to the pub. Apparently John had agreed to submit to hypnosis. This was exciting. Although none of us believed that he knew anything of Genette's disappearance, we all wanted to know more about the home background. Bob Cracknell was convinced that Genette was upset and unhappy that day as she cycled off to collect the newspapers. If so, it would tend to confirm a theory I have long held: that depression and low spirits play an important part in 'victimology'; unhappy people are accident-prone. Now, at least, we might have a chance to find out something about the background to Genette's disappearance.

Half an hour later, the Tate family, and Tania's boyfriend, David, drove back with me to Newton Poppleford. It was clear that they felt that being willing to submit to hypnosis might throw some light on Genette's disappearance, and they were eager to try anything. The first thing Joe Keeton did was to test all three of them for 'hypnotisableness'. Tania responded as well as Margaret had. So did John. (Here Joe used a different test, telling him to lock his fingers with his eyes closed — then telling him that they were jammed and would not come apart. John did not finally succeed in pulling them apart until told to do so, and the effort was obviously tremendous.) Neither test worked on Vi. She pulled her hands apart instantly; and in the 'book test', the two hands remained on the same level throughout. She was apparently completely unhypnotisable — although she insisted that she was not deliberately resisting.

For the next half hour, Joe hypnotised Tania — Genette's pretty sixteen-year-old step-sister. Tania described in detail the day of Genette's disappearance, from the moment she woke up in the morning. Nothing unusual seems to have taken place, except that John and Tania indulged in a little horse-play, and Genette walked into the room as this was happening. Tania insisted that she was amused rather than upset. John's relations with Tania were affectionate, and there was nothing unusual in them 'larking about'. Sometime after midday, John, Tania and David left Aylesbeare to collect Vi at the hospital, and take Tania to the bus station. The bus was half an hour late, so it was not until after three that John and Vi Tate were able to drive back to Aylesbeare. By the time they arrived, the two girls had already raised the alarm about Genette's disappearance.

There was nothing new here either — but we had not expected to learn anything new from Tania. Now it was

John's turn. But he obviously felt awkward with his wife and step-daughter in the room. I took the two women downstairs for a drink, while Joe tried to hypnotise John. We went back a quarter of an hour later, and John was wide awake. He had 'gone under' without much trouble, but had awakened with a start within a few minutes when Joe mentioned memory. Clearly, he felt tense in a room full of people. I also suspect that there may have been an element of resistance there. He is an intelligent man, something of a bookworm; he may have felt vaguely that being hypnotised was somehow humiliating, a surrender of his powers of intelligent thought. At all events, it was obviously hopeless. It was now six o'clock, and I had a two-hour drive ahead of me; so I drove the Tates back to Aylesbeare, declined the offer to go in for a drink, and went on home.

The investigation was still, as far as I could see, marking time — unless one of the car licence numbers given by Margaret and Tracey proved to be correct. But I was inclined to doubt it. I would have been more convinced if both had given the same number. In fact, a check with the car licensing records revealed that neither number existed.

At least there had been one minor breakthrough since my last visit. Dick had spent an evening with Chief Superintendent Rundle, and had finally convinced him that we were not out for money or publicity. The evening had ended in a friendly atmosphere, with Mr. Rundle offering us maximum co-operation. He was to prove as good as his word.

I was back in Aylesbeare again two days later. One of our clairvoyants — probably Nella — had pinpointed a plantation of trees as the place where Genette's body had been concealed. This seemed plausible; it was within a mile of Aylesbeare, and could be reached by turning right towards Aylesbeare Common — out of Within Lane — then left towards Ottery St Mary. Andrew decided to mount another full-scale search, and asked for volunteers. This again had the effect of alienating Mr Rundle's goodwill; he felt he should have been consulted. Besides, the plantation had already been thoroughly searched, and he felt that this repetition was a reflection on the police. With some difficulty, Andrew succeeded in convincing him that there was no implied criticism of the police — we were simply pursuing our own method of research, which involved following up the 'impressions' of clairvoyants.

Since the search was scheduled for a Sunday, my wife and our two boys — aged six and thirteen — came with me to Aylesbeare. It had been raining heavily, so we all took boots. The Village Hall was crowded, and ladies from the WVS were serving soup. Someone had lent the team a personnel carrier — a low, eight-wheeled vehicle that could plough through any conditions — and we all crowded into it. The first stop was a local farm, where one of our clairvoyants said we would find some article of Genette's clothing. The farmer, apparently, was hostile, and we expected him to come bursting out of the farmhouse as we went past; but all was quiet — perhaps he was helping in the search. We halted in a narrow, waterlogged lane, and peered into the hedgerows while Andrew plodded across the fields to contact a team of marines who were scouring the ditches. When he returned — with no developments to report — we drove on to the plantation. Here there were such enormous crowds beating their way through the undergrowth that our presence was obviously superfluous. Someone here had found a belt — a muddy object that was handed over to the police. I looked at it, but it was clearly not the kind of thing Genette would have worn to keep up her trousers. A man's hat was also discovered. The finding of these objects was later reported on television as if it might be a major breakthrough; in fact, the finds led nowhere. Towards mid-afternoon, the children were so wet and muddy that I decided that we should go home.

I was back again the following day — although by now, I have to admit that I was beginning to find all this driving exhausting. The odd thing was that, in spite of the fatigue — and the total lack of any kind of breakthrough — there was an underlying sense of purpose that kept us all alert. Everyone knows the feeling: when you've lost something, and searched for it without success, and suddenly you say 'Damn it, it's *got* to be here somewhere ...', and begin a new and thorough search, which often uncovers the object. We felt the same. Genette *had* to be somewhere, and there was a fifty-fifty chance she was still in the area. And with a little luck, we might find a clue in a place no one had bothered to search thoroughly.

Besides, Nella had laid her head on the block, and said that she felt strongly that Genette would be found within the next day or so. Everyone on the team hoped that he might be the one to make some crucial discovery. This is why, in spite of the cold, and the lack of result so far, no one seemed discouraged or cynical.

I found the usual pile of letters and telephone messages waiting for me at the Incident Centre. There was also a new lead, more bizarre than anything so far. A local housewife — whom I shall call Jean — had been sitting with a pencil in her hand, making a sketch, when the pencil began to write of its own accord. It wrote: 'Genette, Genette, Genette ...' several times, then 'Help me'. Jean was startled and shaken. She asked out loud: 'Is that Genette Tate?', and the pencil wrote 'Yes'. In answer to more questions, 'Genette' said that she had been carried away by a man in a car. She had been taken, she said, to a wood, and dumped in a stream. Later, her body had been moved. One of her sandals, she said (although Genette had been wearing plimsolls), would be found near the spot.

Jean had been thoroughly upset by all this. Like everyone else in the area, she had thought a great deal about Genette's disappearance, and wondered how she would react if it was her own child. Now she was inclined to believe that her unconscious mind was playing tricks. She asked Genette if she could draw her attacker (Genette was a competent artist, to judge by a picture we had in the file), and the pencil drew a sinister-looking man, with staring eyes. Jean found it so horrifying that she was unable to look at it for more than a few seconds. Jean then took a map of the area, and asked 'Genette' to mark the spot where she had been taken. The pencil unhesitatingly drew a circle on Aylesbeare Common, half a mile east of the Halfway House. At this point, she decided to contact our research unit.

Jean was a pale girl in her late twenties. She had read one of my books, and particularly wanted to talk to me. I took her through her story, looked at the drawing of the man, at the paper with the handwriting (to my eyes, it was not much like Genette's), and at the map. The obvious thing was to search the area on Aylesbeare Common. Jean told me she had already been there, and had found the spot somehow 'nasty' — so much so that she had to hurry away.

I was interested to note that there *was* a place called Broad Oak on the edge of the Common close to Aylesbeare — the name Bob Cracknell had mentioned on our first visit. The map showed a track leading from Broad Oak on to the Common. This fitted in with my own theory, that whoever had taken Genette knew the area, and made straight for the Common as soon as he had her safely in the car. But the spot marked by Jean's invisible informant was much further to the east, and had to be approached from the Sidmouth road. I found myself wondering whether there might be an old track from Broad Oak to the spot marked on the map. The only way to find out was to go and look.

We drove on to the Common along a newly asphalted farm road. The farmer, apparently, had already reacted with fury when one of our team called on him, on the grounds that he didn't want our vehicles wearing out his road — a curious attitude, since asphalt is fairly durable. But the day was wet and cold, with sudden heavy showers, and I had no intention of leaving the car at the public carpark, on the main road. We parked in a muddy turning-place, and walked down the hill. The spot marked on the map was a ten-minute walk. It *was* fairly close to a farm track, although it was a remote and lonely spot — not, according to Jean, the kind of place frequented by visitors, even on a hot August afternoon. The ground was covered with bracken, and there were some fallen trees. I began to make a fairly thorough search of the area, tramping through the undergrowth, moving backward and forward in a zig-zag line. I was not hoping to find a body — the previous search team would have already located it — but the sandal or plimsoll might easily have been overlooked, underneath a log or under a bush. There was nothing. When I got back to Jean, she was looking pale and upset. 'I can't stand this place. It gives me a horrible sensation. I *know* something happened here.' She looked as if she might faint. So we moved on. It began to rain — so heavily that we had to take shelter. Even so, both of us were soaked. When it stopped, I ploughed through the bushes and bracken to the west, to see whether this spot *could* be reached by car from Broad Oak. It was soon apparent that the answer was no; there was a valley in between. Which knocked a hole in my theory that there might be a connection between Jean's automatic writing and Bob Cracknell's 'impression' that Genette had been taken to Broad Oak.

It was now halfway through December, and we seemed to be running out of leads. Andrew had decided to wind up the Special Research Unit at Christmas. I could think of only two possibilities. One was to ask Bob Cracknell to come and take another look at the terrain, and see if he came up with any new impressions. The other was to contact a dowser friend, Bill Lewis, who lived in Wales. Bill has a reputation as one of the best dowsers in Britain — perhaps in Europe. His health has been poor in recent years, and there was no chance of getting him to come all the way to Aylesbeare. But he has also had a great deal of success at 'map dowsing'. No one can explain why map dowsing should work — that is, why a diviner should be able to locate water on a map just as easily as on an actual site. It certainly defies all the laws of logic — at least, if we assume that the divining rod responds to some kind of electrical vibration or emanation from water. But then, few dowsers hold that particular theory — for the simple reason that they know they can 'tune in' to anything they like. A good dowser can find literally anything. I could hide a penny and a fifty-pence piece under the carpet, and a dowser could not only locate them with his rod, but identify which is which — simply by 'tuning in' to the different metals.

It seemed worth trying; so I wrote to Bill Lewis, explaining what we were trying to do, and asking if he would help. He replied immediately, asking for a map of the area and — if possible — a lock of Genette's hair, to enable him to 'tune in'. In fact, we had a lock of her hair, but the Tates were understandably reluctant to entrust it to the post. Andrew decided to drive up and see Bill at Abergavenny. Underestimating the distance from Exeter to south Wales, he arrived around midnight, to the disgust of Mrs Lewis — who nevertheless woke her husband and persuaded him to come downstairs. Bill obligingly swung a pendulum over a map of Devon, and received a strong response from an area about thirty miles from Aylesbeare, north of Crediton. For more exact results, he needed an ordnance survey map of the area, which Andrew promised to send him.

Meanwhile, I had contacted Bob Cracknell and asked him if he could return to Aylesbeare. He arrived early in the morning on Saturday, 16 December, having driven since 4am. I arrived a couple of hours later. We drove immediately up to Aylesbeare Common. I had told him about Jean and her automatic writing, but gave no further details. As we walked along the muddy track, he stopped suddenly. 'Something happened about here. I get a feeling she was brought here.'

It was about ten yards away from the area that Jean found so 'creepy'. 'What do you think happened then?' 'She was buried ... in a field. Is there a field anywhere near?' Andrew crashed through the undergrowth to the right, and peered over a hedge. 'There's a field over here.' Bob followed him, and looked excited. 'Yes, this could be it.' We climbed over into the field, and searched around, looking for any spot that might be a grave. But in the five months since Genette's disappearance, a grave would probably be indistinguishable from the rest of the field. 'We need a helicopter and a good camera.' 'We've got a helicopter', said Andrew, 'We've been lent one.' In fact, a local firm had offered us the use of a helicopter for aerial photography, and one of our team — an expert photographer — had already taken many aerial photographs.

I led Bob back to the spot on the path where he had stopped. To my disappointment, he showed no interest in the area that Jean had indicated. But at least, he had 'felt' something fairly close to it. As it started to rain again, we made our way back to the White Horse to lunch.

Back in Aylesbeare, I saw Vi Tate going into their cottage; I suggested that she might like to come up with us in the helicopter. She liked the idea — she had never been in a helicopter. An hour later, Vi, Bob Cracknell and myself took off from the muddy field opposite the Village Hall. The pilot flew low, and it was easy to locate the road on to Aylesbeare Common. We found the field, and flew around it twice. From the air, there was a spot that looked greener than the rest — close to the area we had searched that morning. We noted its position, then told the pilot to fly back. It was getting dark, and he was low on fuel. I had been hoping that

Bob might receive some more 'impressions' as we flew over the Common; but he told me he felt nothing.

At four o'clock I left the team in the bar of the local pub — we had been ejected from the Village Hall while they held the Christmas Draw — and drove into Exeter to collect my wife, who had been doing the Christmas shopping. It had been an interesting day but — on the whole — once more a waste of time. It seemed to me unlikely that the green patch we had noticed in the field was a grave. If it had been, the earlier search teams would have found it.

I also remembered that Nella's time limit was now up — the period in which she said we would make an important discovery.

I talked to Andrew on the phone the following day. The team had checked the green patch in the field, and driven rods into the turf. Whatever it was, it was not a grave.

On the Tuesday before Christmas, the group was due to break up. I have to admit that the thought gave me nothing but relief. I drove to Aylesbeare around midday. The weather was now icy, and there was a heavy frost. In spite of two heaters, the Village Hall was as cold as a tomb. We sat around a table, and did a last co-ordination of various 'leads'. Most of them had been followed up, with negative results. We had searched in woods, in sewers, in compost heaps, in churchyards, in ponds, in barns, even in a sewage works near Exeter, where a bulldozer had been digging trenches at the time Genette vanished. I had driven to Aylesbeare a dozen times in all — over two thousand miles. Now, three weeks later, we knew as little as when we started.

The team now had a new member — an enthusiastic Hungarian lady named Ilonka, who told us that she had through hypnosis. If Hazel could be induced to remember that car number ...

At home, the following day, I wrote to Joe Keeton, outlining the problem and asking if he would be willing to come down and hypnotise Hazel and the two children. Twenty-four hours later, Joe rang me from Liverpool, saying he'd be happy to help. If Hazel had really memorised the number plate, then it could be recovered under hypnosis, because the memory carries a photographic record of everything we have seen and heard, even unconsciously.

That sounded promising. Joe would come over the following week; he was busy until then. So, for that matter, was I. Andrew was clearly hoping that I would go to stay at the Halfway House and take a more active part in the search; but he obviously had no idea of the problems of an overworked writer. On the day I arrived back from Aylesbeare, the *New York Times* had phoned me to ask if I could produce a 2,500-word article on Bernard Shaw and Feminism before the weekend. I was supposed to be writing a three-act play for the Ty Coch Theatre Company in Cardiff, to be presented at the end of January, and I had so far written only the first act — the play was going into rehearsal in three week's time. I was being nagged by my publisher to revise a book on Wilhelm Reich, and by the BBC to finish a long novel which was to be serialised as a television play. Andrew was obviously disappointed that I wasn't there, on the spot; but then, Andrew worked only half the year as a TV producer, and spent the other half 'resting'. Anyway, the whole project struck me as oddly pointless and aimless. Of course, *if* we succeeded in finding Genette, everybody would congratulate him on a brilliant hunch. But, as far as I could see, our chances were minimal; the police had already done the real work.

Still, I kept my doubts to myself. And a week later, with the article and another half-act of the play completed, I drove back to Aylesbeare, to watch Joe Keeton in action.

In fact, Joe had arrived there on the previous day; I had been in hospital for my annual check-up, so could not attend. But it seemed that I hadn't missed much. He had been along to Hazel's home to try and hypnotise her, but it had been impossible. She had been too tense and nervous; after an hour, Joe had been forced to give up.

When I arrived — at a pub in Newton Poppleford where the session was due to take place — Margaret was already there. She was an intelligent little girl, younger than Tracey. There were also half a dozen other people present in the sitting-room over the public bar. These included Andrew Wilson and Dick Lee, a policeman and a doctor — the latter was present to provide medical supervision — and two secretaries. Joe Keeton, a large reassuring man with a north-country accent, was already talking when I arrived. He was explaining to Margaret about hypnosis — that it was not some kind of magic, or an infallible lie detector, but merely an attempt to get through to her unconscious mind, to find out things it had forgotten. It was like watching a stage entertainment; we all sat there, completely absorbed.

First of all, said Joe, he was going to try a simple experiment to see if Margaret was a good hypnotic subject. He asked her to close her eyes, then stretch out both her hands in front of her, one palm upwards, the other with the thumb pointing to the ceiling. He wanted her to imagine that a large balloon was tied to the thumb, so that the hand could not fall down. Meanwhile, she was to imagine that he had placed a large and heavy book on the palm of the other hand. Now he was going to place another book on it. Then another ... At the mention of each book, Margaret's hand dropped down about an inch. Joe told her to open her eyes and look at her hands. She was obviously startled to see that they were now no longer parallel.

Having established that Margaret was a good subject, Joe said he now intended to try another experiment. He was going to give Margaret a secret refuge, a place where she could go whenever she felt tired or miserable. What kind of a place would she like? A wooded valley? A shady stream? A beach? Margaret decided for the beach. Then Joe proceeded to hypnotise her. 'I want you to close your eyes and put your hands beside you. You're feeling completely comfortable and relaxed. You're so relaxed you feel as if you could drift off to sleep. Your body feels heavy, very heavy, and your eyelids are so heavy that you can't open them. Try to open them. You see ... you can't. As I count to ten you'll fall into a deep sleep. One, two ...' Soon, Margaret's regular breathing convinced us she was asleep. To our amusement, one of the secretaries had also dropped off to sleep. Joe then told Margaret that she was at the top of a flight of three steps leading down to a door. She would walk down the steps as he counted to three, then open the door. Then she would find herself a sunny beach, all alone, with the breakers splashing on the sand. We watched Margaret as she obeyed an order to wiggle her toes in the sand, then turn her face up towards the sunlight. Finally, Joe told her that he was going to write down a sentence on a sheet of paper — *her* own sentence, which would always enable her to go back to the beach whenever she wanted. She would have to repeat the words in exactly this order (otherwise, said Joe, it would be too easy, and she might accidentally hypnotise herself in some unsuitable situation) — and he wrote them down on a sheet of paper. 'I am now going to my beach for X minutes (she was to insert the number herself), and when I wake up I shall feel relaxed and completely refreshed.'

At this point Joe roused her from the trance. Then he handed her the sheet of paper on which he had written the words. She read it, closed her eyes, and immediately went to sleep again. A few minutes later she woke up, with a bright, charming smile; in answer to Joe's question, she said she felt marvellous. She had been back to her beach.

It was now time to get down to the serious business. Once again, Joe placed her in a trance. Then he told her: 'It is the afternoon of Saturday the 19th of August, earlier this year. The time is now three o'clock. Where are you?' 'In Within Lane.' 'And who is with you?' 'Tracey …' Step by step, Joe took her along the lane to the bridge, making her repeat the conversation. If Dick or I wanted to ask a question, we only had to catch Joe's eye and interpose; Margaret answered us as readily as Joe. We asked her about the sounds she could hear — she mentioned a tractor in a field over to the left. She described Genette riding up to them as they walked back up the hill from the bridge, and the conversation about the newspaper as Genette walked beside them. She described the car that went past them — so they had to stand in to the side of the lane. Joe asked her who was driving; she said she couldn't see —

she wasn't looking. Joe told her to look now, and she said she saw a middle-aged couple. He asked her to look down at the licence plate and read it. She read out a number, slowly and deliberately. We glanced at one another, hoping that this might be the breakthrough we all hoped for. Dick interrupted to ask whether she and Tracey left the lane at any point, even for a moment. Did they, perhaps, climb over a gate to 'spend a penny'? Margaret firmly denied this. And she also denied seeing a second car. She went on to describe finding the bicycle, calling Genette's name, looking over the hedge into the field, then into the opposite field. (For some reason, neither of them thought to look up the track a few yards back along the lane — by the field Bob Cracknell said the man had dragged Genette into.)

Finally, Joe woke her up. On the whole, it had been disappointing. Margaret had answered every question fully. But except for the car number, she had not told us anything that she had not already told Dick and me as we walked with her along Within Lane.

It was now getting close to lunch time. Margaret and her mother left. Tracey was due after lunch. While we waited, the girls asked Joe if he could give them a 'beach' too. Both proved to be excellent hypnotic subjects; within a few minutes, both were breathing deeply, wearing beautific smiles as they wiggled their toes in the sand and turned their faces up to the sun.

Later, it was Tracey's turn. She struck me as tense and nervous. Although only fourteen, she seemed much more grown-up than Margaret, a young lady with her own ideas, and a will of her own. She was harder to hypnotise than Margaret, but after ten minutes she seemed relaxed enough. I found myself wondering whether she was genuinely asleep, or whether she was pretending, simply to oblige us. There was no way of telling. Hypnotised people do not speak in a slow, dreamy voice; they sound very much as they do when awake. Again, Joe took her over the same ground as Margaret; the walk along Within Lane to the bridge, the conversation with Genette and the two holidaymakers. When the car passed, she was also asked to look through the windscreen. She said the driver was a man, and that he was alone. She also read the number plate, figure by figure; we all noticed that she gave a different number from the one Margaret had read aloud. The police sergeant noted down everything she said. The rest of us were beginning to feel that all this effort was leading nowhere. Like Margaret, Tracey told us nothing that we did not already know.

I offered to drive Tracey and her mother back to Aylesbeare. And at this point, Andrew asked me to call on John Tate, and bring him back to the pub. Apparently John had agreed to submit to hypnosis. This was exciting. Although none of us believed that he knew anything of Genette's disappearance, we all wanted to know more about the home background. Bob Cracknell was convinced that Genette was upset and unhappy that day as she cycled off to collect the newspapers. If so, it would tend to confirm a theory I have long held: that depression and low spirits play an important part in 'victimology'; unhappy people are accident-prone. Now, at least, we might have a chance to find out something about the background to Genette's disappearance.

Half an hour later, the Tate family, and Tania's boyfriend, David, drove back with me to Newton Poppleford. It was clear that they felt that being willing to submit to hypnosis might throw some light on Genette's disappearance, and they were eager to try anything. The first thing Joe Keeton did was to test all three of them for 'hypnotisableness'. Tania responded as well as Margaret had. So did John. (Here Joe used a different test, telling him to lock his fingers with his eyes closed — then telling him that they were jammed and would not come apart. John did not finally succeed in pulling them apart until told to do so, and the effort was obviously tremendous.) Neither test worked on Vi. She pulled her hands apart instantly; and in the 'book test', the two hands remained on the same level throughout. She was apparently completely unhypnotisable — although she insisted that she was not deliberately resisting.

For the next half hour, Joe hypnotised Tania — Genette's pretty sixteen-year-old step-sister. Tania described in detail the day of Genette's disappearance, from the moment she woke up in the morning. Nothing unusual seems to have taken place, except that John and Tania indulged in a little horse-play, and Genette walked into the room as this was happening. Tania insisted that she was amused rather than upset. John's relations with Tania were affectionate, and there was nothing unusual in them 'larking about'. Sometime after midday, John, Tania and David left Aylesbeare to collect Vi at the hospital, and take Tania to the bus station. The bus was half an hour late, so it was not until after three that John and Vi Tate were able to drive back to Aylesbeare. By the time they arrived, the two girls had already raised the alarm about Genette's disappearance.

There was nothing new here either — but we had not expected to learn anything new from Tania. Now it was

John's turn. But he obviously felt awkward with his wife and step-daughter in the room. I took the two women downstairs for a drink, while Joe tried to hypnotise John. We went back a quarter of an hour later, and John was wide awake. He had 'gone under' without much trouble, but had awakened with a start within a few minutes when Joe mentioned memory. Clearly, he felt tense in a room full of people. I also suspect that there may have been an element of resistance there. He is an intelligent man, something of a bookworm; he may have felt vaguely that being hypnotised was somehow humiliating, a surrender of his powers of intelligent thought. At all events, it was obviously hopeless. It was now six o'clock, and I had a two-hour drive ahead of me; so I drove the Tates back to Aylesbeare, declined the offer to go in for a drink, and went on home.

The investigation was still, as far as I could see, marking time — unless one of the car licence numbers given by Margaret and Tracey proved to be correct. But I was inclined to doubt it. I would have been more convinced if both had given the same number. In fact, a check with the car licensing records revealed that neither number existed.

At least there had been one minor breakthrough since my last visit. Dick had spent an evening with Chief Superintendent Rundle, and had finally convinced him that we were not out for money or publicity. The evening had ended in a friendly atmosphere, with Mr. Rundle offering us maximum co-operation. He was to prove as good as his word.

I was back in Aylesbeare again two days later. One of our clairvoyants — probably Nella — had pinpointed a plantation of trees as the place where Genette's body had been concealed. This seemed plausible; it was within a mile of Aylesbeare, and could be reached by turning right towards Aylesbeare Common — out of Within Lane — then left towards Ottery St Mary. Andrew decided to mount another full-scale search, and asked for volunteers. This again had the effect of alienating Mr Rundle's goodwill; he felt he should have been consulted. Besides, the plantation had already been thoroughly searched, and he felt that this repetition was a reflection on the police. With some difficulty, Andrew succeeded in convincing him that there was no implied criticism of the police — we were simply pursuing our own method of research, which involved following up the 'impressions' of clairvoyants.

Since the search was scheduled for a Sunday, my wife and our two boys — aged six and thirteen — came with me to Aylesbeare. It had been raining heavily, so we all took boots. The Village Hall was crowded, and ladies from the WVS were serving soup. Someone had lent the team a personnel carrier — a low, eight-wheeled vehicle that could plough through any conditions — and we all crowded into it. The first stop was a local farm, where one of our clairvoyants said we would find some article of Genette's clothing. The farmer, apparently, was hostile, and we expected him to come bursting out of the farmhouse as we went past; but all was quiet — perhaps he was helping in the search. We halted in a narrow, waterlogged lane, and peered into the hedgerows while Andrew plodded across the fields to contact a team of marines who were scouring the ditches. When he returned — with no developments to report — we drove on to the plantation. Here there were such enormous crowds beating their way through the undergrowth that our presence was obviously superfluous. Someone here had found a belt — a muddy object that was handed over to the police. I looked at it, but it was clearly not the kind of thing Genette would have worn to keep up her trousers. A man's hat was also discovered. The finding of these objects was later reported on television as if it might be a major breakthrough; in fact, the finds led nowhere. Towards mid-afternoon, the children were so wet and muddy that I decided that we should go home.

I was back again the following day — although by now, I have to admit that I was beginning to find all this driving exhausting. The odd thing was that, in spite of the fatigue — and the total lack of any kind of breakthrough — there was an underlying sense of purpose that kept us all alert. Everyone knows the feeling: when you've lost something, and searched for it without success, and suddenly you say 'Damn it, it's *got* to be here somewhere ...', and begin a new and thorough search, which often uncovers the object. We felt the same. Genette *had* to be somewhere, and there was a fifty-fifty chance she was still in the area. And with a little luck, we might find a clue in a place no one had bothered to search thoroughly.

Besides, Nella had laid her head on the block, and said that she felt strongly that Genette would be found within the next day or so. Everyone on the team hoped that he might be the one to make some crucial discovery. This is why, in spite of the cold, and the lack of result so far, no one seemed discouraged or cynical.

I found the usual pile of letters and telephone messages waiting for me at the Incident Centre. There was also a new lead, more bizarre than anything so far. A local housewife — whom I shall call Jean — had been sitting with a pencil in her hand, making a sketch, when the pencil began to write of its own accord. It wrote: 'Genette, Genette, Genette ...' several times, then 'Help me'. Jean was startled and shaken. She asked out loud: 'Is that Genette Tate?', and the pencil wrote 'Yes'. In answer to more questions, 'Genette' said that she had been carried away by a man in a car. She had been taken, she said, to a wood, and dumped in a stream. Later, her body had been moved. One of her sandals, she said (although Genette had been wearing plimsolls), would be found near the spot.

Jean had been thoroughly upset by all this. Like everyone else in the area, she had thought a great deal about Genette's disappearance, and wondered how she would react if it was her own child. Now she was inclined to believe that her unconscious mind was playing tricks. She asked Genette if she could draw her attacker (Genette was a competent artist, to judge by a picture we had in the file), and the pencil drew a sinister-looking man, with staring eyes. Jean found it so horrifying that she was unable to look at it for more than a few seconds. Jean then took a map of the area, and asked 'Genette' to mark the spot where she had been taken. The pencil unhesitatingly drew a circle on Aylesbeare Common, half a mile east of the Halfway House. At this point, she decided to contact our research unit.

Jean was a pale girl in her late twenties. She had read one of my books, and particularly wanted to talk to me. I took her through her story, looked at the drawing of the man, at the paper with the handwriting (to my eyes, it was not much like Genette's), and at the map. The obvious thing was to search the area on Aylesbeare Common. Jean told me she had already been there, and had found the spot somehow 'nasty' — so much so that she had to hurry away.

I was interested to note that there *was* a place called Broad Oak on the edge of the Common close to Aylesbeare — the name Bob Cracknell had mentioned on our first visit. The map showed a track leading from Broad Oak on to the Common. This fitted in with my own theory, that whoever had taken Genette knew the area, and made straight for the Common as soon as he had her safely in the car. But the spot marked by Jean's invisible informant was much further to the east, and had to be approached from the Sidmouth road. I found myself wondering whether there might be an old track from Broad Oak to the spot marked on the map. The only way to find out was to go and look.

We drove on to the Common along a newly asphalted farm road. The farmer, apparently, had already reacted with fury when one of our team called on him, on the grounds that he didn't want our vehicles wearing out his road — a curious attitude, since asphalt is fairly durable. But the day was wet and cold, with sudden heavy showers, and I had no intention of leaving the car at the public carpark, on the main road. We parked in a muddy turning-place, and walked down the hill. The spot marked on the map was a ten-minute walk. It *was* fairly close to a farm track, although it was a remote and lonely spot — not, according to Jean, the kind of place frequented by visitors, even on a hot August afternoon. The ground was covered with bracken, and there were some fallen trees. I began to make a fairly thorough search of the area, tramping through the undergrowth, moving backward and forward in a zig-zag line. I was not hoping to find a body — the previous search team would have already located it — but the sandal or plimsoll might easily have been overlooked, underneath a log or under a bush. There was nothing. When I got back to Jean, she was looking pale and upset. 'I can't stand this place. It gives me a horrible sensation. I *know* something happened here.' She looked as if she might faint. So we moved on. It began to rain — so heavily that we had to take shelter. Even so, both of us were soaked. When it stopped, I ploughed through the bushes and bracken to the west, to see whether this spot *could* be reached by car from Broad Oak. It was soon apparent that the answer was no; there was a valley in between. Which knocked a hole in my theory that there might be a connection between Jean's automatic writing and Bob Cracknell's 'impression' that Genette had been taken to Broad Oak.

It was now halfway through December, and we seemed to be running out of leads. Andrew had decided to wind up the Special Research Unit at Christmas. I could think of only two possibilities. One was to ask Bob Cracknell to come and take another look at the terrain, and see if he came up with any new impressions. The other was to contact a dowser friend, Bill Lewis, who lived in Wales. Bill has a reputation as one of the best dowsers in Britain — perhaps in Europe. His health has been poor in recent years, and there was no chance of getting him to come all the way to Aylesbeare. But he has also had a great deal of success at 'map dowsing'. No one can explain why map dowsing should work — that is, why a diviner should be able to locate water on a map just as easily as on an actual site. It certainly defies all the laws of logic — at least, if we assume that the divining rod responds to some kind of electrical vibration or emanation from water. But then, few dowsers hold that particular theory — for the simple reason that they know they can 'tune in' to anything they like. A good dowser can find literally anything. I could hide a penny and a fifty-pence piece under the carpet, and a dowser could not only locate them with his rod, but identify which is which — simply by 'tuning in' to the different metals.

It seemed worth trying; so I wrote to Bill Lewis, explaining what we were trying to do, and asking if he would help. He replied immediately, asking for a map of the area and — if possible — a lock of Genette's hair, to enable him to 'tune in'. In fact, we had a lock of her hair, but the Tates were understandably reluctant to entrust it to the post. Andrew decided to drive up and see Bill at Abergavenny. Underestimating the distance from Exeter to south Wales, he arrived around midnight, to the disgust of Mrs Lewis — who nevertheless woke her husband and persuaded him to come downstairs. Bill obligingly swung a pendulum over a map of Devon, and received a strong response from an area about thirty miles from Aylesbeare, north of Crediton. For more exact results, he needed an ordnance survey map of the area, which Andrew promised to send him.

Meanwhile, I had contacted Bob Cracknell and asked him if he could return to Aylesbeare. He arrived early in the morning on Saturday, 16 December, having driven since 4am. I arrived a couple of hours later. We drove immediately up to Aylesbeare Common. I had told him about Jean and her automatic writing, but gave no further details. As we walked along the muddy track, he stopped suddenly. 'Something happened about here. I get a feeling she was brought here.'

It was about ten yards away from the area that Jean found so 'creepy'. 'What do you think happened then?' 'She was buried ... in a field. Is there a field anywhere near?' Andrew crashed through the undergrowth to the right, and peered over a hedge. 'There's a field over here.' Bob followed him, and looked excited. 'Yes, this could be it.' We climbed over into the field, and searched around, looking for any spot that might be a grave. But in the five months since Genette's disappearance, a grave would probably be indistinguishable from the rest of the field. 'We need a helicopter and a good camera.' 'We've got a helicopter', said Andrew, 'We've been lent one.' In fact, a local firm had offered us the use of a helicopter for aerial photography, and one of our team — an expert photographer — had already taken many aerial photographs.

I led Bob back to the spot on the path where he had stopped. To my disappointment, he showed no interest in the area that Jean had indicated. But at least, he had 'felt' something fairly close to it. As it started to rain again, we made our way back to the White Horse to lunch.

Back in Aylesbeare, I saw Vi Tate going into their cottage; I suggested that she might like to come up with us in the helicopter. She liked the idea — she had never been in a helicopter. An hour later, Vi, Bob Cracknell and myself took off from the muddy field opposite the Village Hall. The pilot flew low, and it was easy to locate the road on to Aylesbeare Common. We found the field, and flew around it twice. From the air, there was a spot that looked greener than the rest — close to the area we had searched that morning. We noted its position, then told the pilot to fly back. It was getting dark, and he was low on fuel. I had been hoping that

Bob might receive some more 'impressions' as we flew over the Common; but he told me he felt nothing.

At four o'clock I left the team in the bar of the local pub — we had been ejected from the Village Hall while they held the Christmas Draw — and drove into Exeter to collect my wife, who had been doing the Christmas shopping. It had been an interesting day but — on the whole — once more a waste of time. It seemed to me unlikely that the green patch we had noticed in the field was a grave. If it had been, the earlier search teams would have found it.

I also remembered that Nella's time limit was now up — the period in which she said we would make an important discovery.

I talked to Andrew on the phone the following day. The team had checked the green patch in the field, and driven rods into the turf. Whatever it was, it was not a grave.

On the Tuesday before Christmas, the group was due to break up. I have to admit that the thought gave me nothing but relief. I drove to Aylesbeare around midday. The weather was now icy, and there was a heavy frost. In spite of two heaters, the Village Hall was as cold as a tomb. We sat around a table, and did a last co-ordination of various 'leads'. Most of them had been followed up, with negative results. We had searched in woods, in sewers, in compost heaps, in churchyards, in ponds, in barns, even in a sewage works near Exeter, where a bulldozer had been digging trenches at the time Genette vanished. I had driven to Aylesbeare a dozen times in all — over two thousand miles. Now, three weeks later, we knew as little as when we started.

The team now had a new member — an enthusiastic Hungarian lady named Ilonka, who told us that she had been Winston Churchill's clairvoyant. Andrew and Ilonka had driven up to Bristol the previous day to see Genette's real mother, and both had found it an upsetting experience. From what they told me, I was glad I hadn't gone with them. Genette's mother was still shattered by her daughter's disappearance, and inclined to blame herself — although she had been eighty miles away at the time. It struck me then that although I had been involved in the search for three weeks, I had never come close to the real tragedy of her disappearance. The only time when Genette had become, for a brief moment, a real person was when I was looking through her school notebooks. They were just like the notebooks of my own children; for a moment, I experienced a sense of anger and bewilderment. She *was* a real child who had been leading a normal existence only a few months ago; then someone had snatched her away from her usual surroundings. It seemed so pointless, so stupid.

Ilonka was convinced that Genette had been knocked off her bicycle by a car, and assured us that if we examined the left-hand pedal, we would see signs of the impact. I told her that I had examined the bicycle closely, and there was no sign of impact. She told me I was wrong, and that I would find that the pedal *was* bent at a slight angle.

Andrew showed me a letter he had received from Bill Lewis. Bill had tried his pendulum over an ordnance survey map of the area north of Crediton. He had received a powerful and unmistakable reaction above a field just outside a village called Poughill. He had marked the field clearly on the map.

This, at least, was quite unambiguous — unlike most of the information we had received. We ate a sandwich lunch, and then drove off to Poughill — Andrew, myself, and a girl named Alex, a university student who had been acting as general co-ordinator and filing clerk. The lanes proved to be narrow and tortuous, and it was getting dark when we arrived. We located the farm — a dog rushed out barking at us — and found a young man on a tractor, who turned out to be the farmer's son. When we explained what we wanted, he gave us permission to search in the field. At this point, Andrew recollected that he had forgotten to bring a spade, or any other tool; the farmer's son lent us a fork. I had brought gumboots, but they proved to be unnecessary. The mud was frozen solid. We walked slowly across the top of the field, peering at the ground. The farmer's son assured us that there was nothing that looked even remotely like a grave, but he proved to be mistaken; within twenty yards of the gate we found an oblong patch about five feet long, where the earth had been disturbed. For a moment, I experienced intense excitement. Was it possible that, after so much fruitless search, we had found what we were looking for? I set to work with the fork. But six inches down, it was obvious that this was no grave; the ground was hard and undisturbed. We plodded on into the next field, digging in a few more places where the earth looked loose. Bill Lewis had said that his pendulum had responded over the top half of the field; but there was nothing else that looked remotely like a grave. I made a deliberate effort to galvanise my flagging attention, and walked slowly down the field, looking for the slightest sign of disturbance. Then, as darkness began to fall, we gave up. Cold and now very hungry, we drove back to Aylesbeare. Our last lead had given out.

There was still one thing that bothered me: Ilonka's

insistence that Genette's bicycle would show some indication of an impact. It seemed unlikely; but after following up so many leads, it seemed a pity to leave this one unchecked. So on the way home, I stopped at the Heavitree Police Station in Exeter, and asked to see Don Crabb. When I told him why I was there, he led me up to a small room at the top of the building; there, leaning against boxes full of files, stood Genette's blue bicycle. We placed it in the centre of the room, and looked at the left pedal. There was not the slightest sign of bending. We looked over the rest of the bicycle inch by inch, until we were convinced that no mark or scratch had been overlooked. I thanked Don Crabb, and went back to my car. At least the case had followed a consistent pattern. Every clue had led nowhere.

I agree that, for sceptics, the lesson of our investigation would seem to be that clairvoyants are a waste of time. But then, the sceptic's view is based on the assumption that 'paranormal cognition' cannot, by the nature of things, exist; and here I cannot agree. In the mid-nineteenth century, an American professor named Buchanan discovered that his students could distinguish various substances even when they were wrapped in brown-paper parcels; his brother-in-law, another professor named Denton, discovered that 'sensitives' could accurately 'read' the history of geological specimens, also wrapped in thick paper. Both concluded that all events somehow 'photograph' themselves on matter, and that human beings possess some crude and undeveloped faculty for 'developing' these impressions. A contemporary Russian scientist, Genady Sergeyev, has invented a machine that can pick up and translate some of these impulses; he claims it proves that emotional energies 'can be assimilated into objects'. (It is described by Henry Gris and William Dick in *The New Soviet Psychic Discoveries*, 1979.) I have worked on a television programme with the Dutch clairvoyant Gerard Croiset, investigating the disappearance of a girl named Pat Macadam, near Glasgow. Here, as in the Genette case, the disappearance remains unsolved. But Croiset's impressions about the site where she vanished — impressions recorded in Utrecht — were so startlingly accurate that none of us had any doubt that some form of paranormal cognition was taking place. Croiset told us that the girl had been murdered in the course of rape, and dumped in the nearby river, off a bridge. The lorry driver with whom she was last seen, has since been sentenced to life imprisonment for a sexual murder; he also admitted to innumerable rapes in the cab of his lorry.

But then, Croiset was operating from Holland; he had no direct involvement in the case. Bob Cracknell, Nella Jones and the other clairvoyants were on the spot. Any 'impressions' they picked up must have been muddled and confused by the tension, the expectation, the theories and suspicions in the minds of those around them. (All clairvoyants admit that they can easily become muddled by telepathic impressions picked up from people around them.) Yet three clairvoyants — Croiset, Cracknell and Nella Jones — all came up with an immediate impression that Genette was dead and under water. This at least shows an interesting unity of opinion.

As to myself, the major lesson of the investigation has been a recognition of how difficult it is to get to grips with reality. I have written extensively of crime, and described police investigations. Like everyone else,

I had imagined the police patiently following up clues, treating the investigation like a problem in mathematics. To be actually involved in such an investigation is to realise that this is completely unlike mathematics — more like blind man's buff. Any question, any search, might lead somewhere; but the odds are a thousand to one. Our search was based upon the assumption that the man who took Genette knew the area, and that her body (for it seems probable she is no longer alive) is still within a ten-mile radius. Yet if I ask myself why I made this assumption, I have to recognise that it was because I found myself unable to envisage a convincing motive. The newspaper photographs of Genette show a tiny, boy-like girl, hardly the type to catch the attention of a sexual psychopath. Therefore, I envisaged the kidnapper as a local man who must have possessed some other motive.

Yet one of these assumptions collapsed as soon as I walked into the Village Hall in December. Recent photographs of Genette lay on the table; these showed her as more grown-up than the familiar police photograph. Dick Lee was also startled by the difference. Why, we wanted to know, was the police photograph so misleading? The answer, it seemed, was that Genette's hair had been cut short a few days before her disappearance; before that, it had been below her shoulders. Therefore, the police asked for a photograph with the short hair style. The only one was of Genette several years earlier. So, in fact, the poster was misleading. Anyone who saw Genette alive after her disappearance may not have recognised her from the photograph.

But the same observation also applies to my assumption about motive. I had been thinking of a child-like figure on the bicycle that afternoon. If I substitute a mental image of a more grown-up teenager, wearing trousers and a sleeveless T-shirt, then it no longer seems impossible that the motive was, quite simply, sexual. And since, in mid-August, the West Country is full of visitors from all over the country, then the assumption that her attacker was a local man loses its plausibility. In fact, even the assumption that it was a man on his own becomes questionable; there have been many cases of sexual attack involving two men. The notion of two men could explain why there seems to have been so little violence or struggle ...

And I must end on that deliberately inconclusive note. This piece can only by concluded if, and when, the mystery of Genette's disappearance is solved.

7   Where is Genette now?

What are we left with; which pieces of this mysterious jigsaw have we been able to put together? What have we discovered and where do we now stand? What can we establish from questioning other people about what happened up to the moment when Genette disappeared that afternoon?

The following is an account of what took place on Saturday, 19 August. In places I have used my imagination to give an impression of what Genette would have been doing, from what we know of her. The times are only approximate because of the many variables involved.

At about 2pm Genette got herself ready and left on her bicycle to collect the newspapers. She would have made a last-minute check around the house, shutting the dog in the kitchen whilst at the same time picking up the cat's food so that the dog couldn't get to it. Then one can imagine her quite happily and contentedly getting her bike out. This was a blue Kahlkoff that we gave her for Christmas, 1977. She would have gone down the two steps outside the back gate, which would have been a little difficult with a bicycle and then cycled off into the village.

On her way she passed one or two people and gave her usual cheery hullo to them as they were her friends. One of these was John Bathard, the normal paperboy, whom she saw just outside the Blue Anchor inn. As she cycled by she shouted across to him: 'My dad wants to see you to talk to you about the paper-round'. We had been discussing it only the night before. Then she turned into the pretty country lane that is Within Lane itself.

In August it is very pretty with the bushes and hedgerows at the height of their growth, the verges a mixture of green grasses and white cow-parsley with dark green bracken pushing through here and there. The hedgerow is rather overgrown making the little lane even narrower. The greenery is interspersed with a few summer flowers. On this particular afternoon the air was still with very little breeze blowing. It was one of the warmest days we had had that summer.

Genette would have cycled along until she came to the junction of Within Lane with the lane that runs from White Cross to Farringdon and then on to Exeter Airport; a sharp left-hand turn here and then a few yards to the junction with the A3052 main road. This was the most dangerous part of her journey and the part that we were most concerned about as the cars moved rather swiftly along this road between Exeter, Sidmouth and the coast. For most of the year there is not so very much traffic here but during the short holiday period it can become one of the busiest in the area with many drivers hurrying along to their holiday destinations, not sure of their route or the road conditions ahead. Genette whilst turning right at this junction had to cross this road and probably had quite a wait for a clear space. She would then have cycled about fifty yards along this road to the White Horse Inn where she picked up the newspapers from the delivery van.

Today she was early because she wanted to collect the balance of the money owing from customers she hadn't seen the day before, and she also wanted to be punctual because people had often teased John Bathard, the usual paperboy, for being late on a Saturday. After all it was the day when the £5 bargain column was published and everyone loves to read this in case it contains something they are looking for. (It is a regular feature in the paper — anyone can advertise free any article they wish to sell for less than £5.)

The newspaper van arrived and the delivery man handed over the papers. It was quite a heavy bundle containing about seventy newspapers. Genette cut the strings securing the bundle, with the small pocket-knife she carried hooked on to her bicycle. Having done this, she put the papers in the pannier on the back of her bicycle. Then she set off delivering newspapers to the bungalows along the main road. This entailed crossing the main road three times and probably took quite some time. She then re-entered Within Lane at approximately 3pm and continued with the paper-round, delivering to the bungalows with long driveways and little cottages standing right on the roadside.

She had delivered altogether fourteen newspapers before she reached the only hill in Within Lane, short but fairly steep, and passed Tracey and Margaret, two of her friends, who were talking to two ladies, who were strangers to her. (These were the two ladies who were later to come forward as having seen these three children together, and who were also to take part in hypnosis sessions.) Genette was forced to dismount and push her bike up the hill as it was too steep to ride. Tracey and Margaret soon caught up and the three of them walked up the hill together. (At this point a car passed them going towards the village.) Then they chatted about a newspaper: Tracey wanted to have her mother's paper and Genette wasn't too happy about it because it hadn't been paid for, but eventually she handed it over and said she would collect the money later.

As the road levelled out Genette remounted her bicycle (time: approximately 3.27pm) and cycled on round the bend out of sight.

The two girls, Tracey and Margaret, sauntered slowly along the lane, reading the newspaper as they went. They were only dawdling and at one time actually put the newspaper down on the road to read it, so you can imagine how still the weather was that afternoon. Eventually they turned the bend and saw Genette's bicycle lying on the ground with newspapers strewn around it. Naturally they were concerned, although at first they thought Genette was playing a prank on them and was perhaps hiding behind the hedge waiting for them. They started calling for her. They climbed up on to the fence, looked over the hedgerows and shouted and called her name, but all to no avail. They came to fetch us but we were not yet home so they returned to Within Lane. En route they met several other children and they all went back to the scene to search.

After a short interval they realised that something was not quite right so one of them started to ride the bicycle home to see if Genette was there, and that was where we met up with Tracey who told us that Genette was missing.

Now, many months later, after all the searches and many hours of questioning, what are we left with as regards the mystery surrounding Genette? We have seven theories and it is possible to add smaller ones in each category. Let us look at each one of these individually. There is no specific order — only the way in which they come to mind.

The first one we thought about was the possibility of Genette running away on her own, either to bring attention to herself or because of some mental disturbance. The reasons why this seems unlikely are varied. They stem from the ordinary everyday things that one would imagine someone would do if they were about to leave home. No preparations were made. She took no clothing with her apart from what she stood up in. The house has been searched on numerous occasions and we now know precisely what she was wearing on that day. Her pocket money was still in its secret hideaway in the house and also in her purse. She could have gone off with the takings from the Friday newspaper-round but this was still a hundred per cent intact. If she had decided to run away she would have had ample opportunity on many other occasions to have done so. She had never run away before nor shown any inclination to do so. As far as we were aware she was happy and she was not the sort of girl one would have expected to run away.

At that time she was looking forward to visiting her mother at the end of the week. She was doing well at school and seemed to be enjoying every minute of it. She was looking forward to a Continental holiday and saving hard towards it. She was also planning to go on a spending spree the following week.

The fact that there have been no sightings of her makes this theory less plausible still. How can it be possible, if she has run away, for her not to have been seen by someone by this time, and surely she would have taken her bicycle with her or at least have ridden it to the nearest bus stop?

The second possibility is that she ran away in collusion with someone. If so, it would again have to have been a spur-of-the-moment decision since she made no preparations, although it is possible that whoever she ran away with told her that they would cope with everything for the future. However, none of her known friends is missing.

During their questioning the police covered a wide circle, visiting every friend we had in Devon and Cornwall and no one was unaccounted for. There is always the possibility that she may have known somebody who was totally out of our circle of friends and unknown in the village and surrounding area. This is, however, unlikely as we were always aware of where she was and what time to expect her home; and in a community like Aylesbeare no one is a stranger for long and someone would have known. We also think that the reward that was being offered would be a big inducement for anyone to make contact.

The third theory, which immediately sprang to my mind at the beginning, was that she had been knocked down by a car, the driver bundling her into his vehicle in a panic, and carrying her off to hospital. There was, however, no damage to the bicycle nor was there any sign of skid marks in the area where it was found. Also the one car that was known to have gone along the lane went past Genette earlier, so if a car had knocked her down it would have had to come from the village; and then turned back with her; otherwise Tracey and Margaret and other witnesses would have seen it. All hospitals were checked and she would have been recognised even if she had been unconscious.

The fourth possibility, a theory put forward by a surprising number of people, is that she was beamed away in a UFO. It is difficult to know what to say ... There is no evidence, but is there ever? Surely, if a UFO had been in the area it would have been sighted by others? There were children only a few hundred yards away from her and a flying object of the size one would imagine a flying saucer to be would be clearly visible for some distance. We are in the realms of the unknown as far as this is concerned.

There had been reports of UFO sightings in the area during the previous week and, in fact, the newspaper Genette was carrying showed a photograph of a supposed sighting above the area. This photograph did bear some resemblance to those taken in Italy in December 1978. There were also the strange burn marks in the field close to where she went from, and the short interruption to our electrical supply on the evening of the same day. Yet to all of these we had been given logical explanations. The photograph showed the landing lights of an aircraft approaching the airport (but what about those over Italy?). The burn marks were caused by some kind of fertiliser (but which fertiliser?). The cut in the electrical supply was caused by a fire at the sub-station (but what caused the fire?). Then there was the odd way that the police behaved every time we mentioned a UFO. They just did not want to discuss it. Yet they would listen to every other theory, however way-out.

There have been many reports of sightings of UFOs over the years, some of them by quite highly trained observers, and enough of them to make one feel that there must be something in it, but after much investigation I can find few reports to suggest that people are spirited away by them. Of those that have been reported, the majority have later turned out to be publicity stunts. So far I have not found one account of a person being taken from the ground and kept. I have, however, read of planes complete with crews disappearing whilst in pursuit of a UFO, but what can one make of reports like that?

Theory number five is that she was sexually assaulted and then murdered. There are a lot of arguments for and against this one. I am against it because anyone in this situation would have thrown the bike over the hedge so that suspicions would not immediately have been roused, allowing more time for a getaway and, of course, where is Genette? After extensive searches in the area there is still no sign of her and no evidence of a struggle having taken place nearby either. There is, of course, the possibility that she was taken out of the area and disposed of in some way or another and this may well have happened. When the search became national we very much relied on people being observant; but some are and some aren't, and because of this no nation-wide search can ever be a satisfactory way of finding someone.

The sixth theory is that she was kidnapped for money. Again, we come back to the lack of evidence of a struggle although, as we have already mentioned, children can all too easily become the victims of a confidence trick and can be persuaded with a few convincing words to get into a stranger's car. But it seems unlikely that she would not have first propped up her bicycle. The bicycle, being the only real piece of evidence, is important in all these theories — we often said in the early days: 'If only that bike could talk!' The other main reason against this theory is that if the motive was money then why has the substantial reward remained unclaimed.

Finally, we come to theory number seven and that is that she was abducted for some reason. Here again the bicycle must count against the theory, but in my mind an abduction seems to be the most likely solution, partly because I feel that she is still alive somewhere. The lack of any positive sighting makes it difficult to believe, but Genette could be anywhere, perhaps in a foreign country where the publicity surrounding her disappearance made little impression.

All that is certain is that someone somewhere holds the solution to this mystery. In time it will be solved. We do not intend to let Genette, or the many other children who go missing each year, be forgotten and just become a statistic in a dusty file.

Our children are our inheritance and our future. They are our dreams and our ambitions. We must take care of them; they are our most valued possessions.

I know, because nothing or no one will ever fill the gap Genette's disappearance has left in our hearts and our lives.

8 International Find a Child

On Monday, 19 February interest began to be shown in the idea we had put forward at a press conference regarding the organisation that we wanted to form to help other people in the same situation as ourselves, and to try to look into the problems associated with missing children.

Over the next few days we appeared on television and we were interviewed on local radio; we were also interviewed for the Jimmy Young show on national radio. We were asked what had given us the idea of starting such an organisation — both the discussions with Pat and Brian Berkshire and the statistics we had read in the newspapers. One report referred to the fact that in 1977 approximately fourteen thousand children under the age of eighteen went missing from their homes — of these a large proportion either returned of their own accord or were found within one or two days. But this statistic made us aware of how large the problem is in Great Britain.

During the months following Genette's disappearance we had followed every single report, either on television newsreels or in the newspapers, of missing children and the problems that this highlighted. We became increasingly concerned about the breakdown in communication between parent and child which was obviously a big factor in these circumstances. We wondered why this situation existed. Was this one of the by-products of children being brought up in an environment where television is a constant companion from birth. Were we giving our children too much and not allowing them enough scope for their instinct for adventure, or teaching them too much too soon? By becoming over-engrossed in our increasingly materialistic lives, were we leaving less and less time for simple conversation with our children? If we are, then to whom are they turning instead — other children, teachers, the make-believe world of the TV screen or complete strangers?

The more we thought about communication, or the lack of it, and its obvious connection with missing children, the more we felt there was a need to do a sociological survey to study the causes of children leaving home. We also felt that if we looked at enough of these cases, of both those children who had been found and those who were still missing, it might be possible to discover some common factors which would enable people to do something constructive about the problem. This, we think, would also help to strengthen the chances of finding some of the missing children.

We called the organisation 'International Find a Child'. Why 'International'? We wanted the organisation to cross national boundaries because there are many situations where it is difficult to get investigations going, simply because of the red tape and political problems that can hamper speedy communication between countries. An independent organisation, we felt, would be able to get round many of these hurdles and follow up leads it had received concerning the possible routes taken by some of the missing children.

One person had taken the trouble to write to us expressing his concern about a possible network of people who were acquiring children for use in brothels and similar establishments in foreign countries. Many people wrote to us regarding the use of children in pornographic literature and films, their feeling being that these children had to come from somewhere, and with the use of drugs, fear, promises and so on, in a strange place, away from their home environment, children could be forced into doing anything. In both these situations (brothels and pornographic material) large and unscrupulous operations could be involved and we felt that some investigation should be done, firstly to prove that such activities are going on and secondly to bring the facts to the public's attention.

The aim of the organisation, we felt, should be to provide help and support when it was needed. When a child goes missing the family needs sympathetic support, ideally from people who know what is like to experience such grief and distress first-hand. We had already decided that we would ourselves offer to do this following our meeting with Pat and Brian Berkshire.

We knew from experience that help was also needed to enable people to grasp the situation going on around them, and to cope with the enormous pressures forced upon them by the Press, the police and sometimes even themselves. These parents are in need of an organisation that can provide practical help by running errands, manning the telephone, doing the shopping and any other necessities that may crop up. It should be possible, in some circumstances, to ease the additional financial burdens brought about by the increased consumption of electricity for heating and lighting, the provision of extra food and drink for visitors, additional travelling expenses for searching, the purchase of special outdoor clothing and so on.

Thus our first aim was to provide comfort and financial assistance, where needed, to the distressed parents of missing children. However, the formation of an organisation able to provide considerable financial assistance would take some time. More immediately, we hoped to be able to set up a network of people in all areas who could be contacted by their own local charitable organisations like the Lions Clubs or Rotarians and who could then be approached for help as and when this became necessary. Trained people would also be available when called upon, even if only as a shoulder to cry on.

The organisation could also undertake research and lobby for new measures and attitudes that would strengthen the chances of finding missing children. Obviously a great deal of research would be needed before the organisation would be in a position to offer advice of any kind, although from our own experiences we could see that there were two worthwhile ideas that could be implemented immediately.

Firstly, the photograph situation. At the moment, so much depends on the parent of a missing child being able to provide an up-to-date professional photograph of their child at a moment's notice. This leaves too much to luck and a more professional approach is needed to beat this tremendous problem. In every field of the fight against crime, sophisticated methods are used. Again, we keep records of our car registration numbers, serial numbers of our bicycles and of various other material objects. As far as the car is concerned, this involves thousands of pounds worth of complicated computer equipment. Yet the most valued possession we all have, our children, have virtually no documentation kept about them.

We feel that the most sensible thing would be to ensure that school photographs are taken on a yearly basis at least, which would enable a photographic record to be built up at the school. It seems the logical thing to do since all the children could be photographed in one place in a relatively short time. Many schools already do this, but not enough, and those schools that do not keep photographic records need only attach a photograph to existing academic records. The police would then know exactly where to find a professional photograph of any child in the country of school age.

Another problem that occurred during Genette's investigation involved a £5 note that had been found in the area with a considerable amount of blood on it. Naturally the police wanted to determine as quickly as possible whether this was Genette's blood. They went to a great deal of trouble in an endeavour to obtain her blood group and found that, although Genette had had many blood tests taken to try to establish whether or not she was a carrier of muscular dystrophy, no record had ever been kept of her blood group. Eventually, by comparing the blood of Sheila and myself, the field was narrowed to several blood group possibilities. Later, on enquiring from our local GP, we found that the only time that the blood group is shown in the medical records is when a patient has an illness associated with blood grouping or prior to an operation where a transfusion may be required. We felt this situation could be very easily remedied by including the blood group on the National Health Service Medical Card — a simple step that could be taken at birth.

Later we realised that there was another advantage to the recording of this information in that rare blood groups would be discovered early in life, whereas now this information only comes to light when a person offers to be a blood donor.

Finally, we felt that a network of people throughout the country could assist by acting independently from the Press and the police in spreading information about missing children through all available outlets. This network would also act as a contact point for families in need of help. The organisation would also collect information so that it could be collated centrally.

Those are the prime aims that seem most worthwhile at present, although time and experience may show that modifications are needed, particularly if we can undertake the kind of research we intend.

We need the help and co-operation of other parents whose children are missing at present and those who have had such an experience in the past. We would want them to make contact with us so that we can learn from their experiences and also so that we can record, to some extent, the sort of things that have happened in their particular situation in the hope that from this we could gain some of the data that is desperately needed in this field.

We also need financial aid to fund the whole thing and to support a period of research. Once our plans became public we wrote to all the national newspapers getting them to publish letters to the Editor telling people all about International Find a Child. Slowly funds began to trickle in. Then we realised that another possible method of raising funds would be to write this book *Genette is Missing*, so we decided that any money we made from the sale of this book would be used to support us while we devoted our entire time to the setting up of the organisation and for work related to the problems of missing children and their families.

That was the beginning of International Find a Child. It began to grow immediately after the Press, TV and radio reported its birth. Now we get a heavy post each day.

We hear from people all over the country and have begun to set up a rather limited network to cover most areas. There are some places from which we have received no offers of help and it is difficult therefore to organise complete coverage. Funds have started to come in and we have built up a small reserve. We began to hear from families who were prepared to assist with research by having their own particular circumstances looked into and recorded in detail, although we treated their communications as confidential, in particular complying with any requests for lack of publicity.

We soon began to become aware of the problems that existed in a field such as this and, in particular, the apparent labelling that is done by the Press or the public at large, which result in conclusions being jumped at and which can often slow up the solving of a missing child problem. Two prime examples of this kind of labelling can be where there is a broken family, as in my own case, when the immediate reaction of public opinion is: oh she has gone to the other parent; and they switch off, having neatly solved the problem satisfactorily for themselves. The other situation concerns children over the age of fifteen; here the immediate conclusion tends to be that he, or she, has run away from home. In fact, unless there is some possibility of a gruesome ending to the story or unless there is some other way the whole thing can be blown up out of all proportion there is not going to be much interest shown. Someone said to me that newspapers have one function: to make money — but surely they have a service to do for the community as well. We were very fortunate with the Press coverage Genette's disappearance received, but some children never even get a mention, particularly in the nationals. We also feel that more TV time could be devoted to the highlighting of missing children. In some areas complete half-hour programmes are given to missing articles like antiques or jewellery, but what is more valuable, people or possessions?

In the future, it will be one of our objectives to endeavour to get every single case of a missing child under the age of eighteen treated in exactly the same way — in other words each case should be treated as if there was a criminal involvement until it is proved otherwise. In this way the criminal would not be given so much leeway or be able to take advantage of the general apathy that exists at present.

We soon became aware that some of the biggest subscribers to these apathetic attitudes were parents and children themselves. Everyone thinks 'it can't possibly happen to me'. The disappearance of Genette from a quiet country lane in the heart of one of the most peaceful areas in Great Britain brought home to us with a bang that we are living in much more violent times than we had appreciated. Our children are in constant danger and so, at times, are we.

We made the 'mistake' of allowing Genette to do a paper-round — something she was very happy doing. At the time when she asked to do it we could only see the benefits: the fresh air and exercise, and something to keep her occupied and out of mischief. We did not see the pitfalls.

We now go about with our eyes more open to the

dangers that parents unthinkingly expose their children to. Have you ever left a child in an unlocked car whilst you have gone into a shop? You can't keep a watch all the time, but it only takes a very few minutes for a child to disappear. Does your child walk to school unaccompanied? If so, it could be several hours before your child is missed. Are you always aware of where your children are and what time they are likely to be home?

These are the situations which the ever growing criminal fringe of society could take advantage of. Children are in need of education on this subject in a more firm and positive way than in the past. They should be warned of all the ploys that could be used to get them into cars and so on. All too easily a child will believe a story told them by a stranger in a car, perhaps that their father has been injured and that the stranger has been asked to come to collect them. Most children will get into the car without a moment's hesitation. Children should be told not to do this under any circumstances whatsoever, unless it is someone they really know. All parents tell their children never to take sweets from a stranger but more needs to be said than that.

We hope that in the future, by continual research, and the dissemination of information, we will be able to prevent at least a few of these children from going missing and remaining missing, so becoming just a statistic. We also hope that International Find a Child, by becoming well known, will discourage the criminal to some extent. These are the directions in which we are going and in which we try to educate the people who become involved with International Find a Child.

If you would like to help financially, please send a donation to

>   International Find a Child
>   c/o Lloyds Bank
>   St Thomas
>   Exeter.

Alternatively, if you would like to help in any other way, then write to me at

>   Barton Farm Cottage
>   Aylesbeare
>   Near Exeter   EX5 2BU.